the Wood-Burning Stove Book

the Wood-Burning Stove Book

GERI HARRINGTON

COLLIER BOOKS
A DIVISION OF MACMILLAN PUBLISHING CO., INC.
NEW YORK
COLLIER MACMILLAN PUBLISHERS
LONDON

TO DON

Macmillan Publishing Co., Inc.
866 Third Avenue, New York, N.Y.
  10022
Collier Macmillan Canada, Ltd.

Library of Congress Cataloging in Publication Data
Harrington, Geri.
  The wood-burning stove book.
  1. Stoves, Wood. I. Title.
TH7438.H36 1977   697'.04   77-7401
ISBN 0-02-080250-1

First Collier Books Edition 1977

The Wood-Burning Stove Book is also published in a hardcover edition by Macmillan Publishing Co., Inc.

Printed in the United States of America

Contents

ACKNOWLEDGMENTS

7

INTRODUCTION

9

1 FROM THE CAVE TO THE COLONIES

17

2 WOOD—THE ECOLOGIST'S FUEL

33

3 HEATING WITH WOOD—DISADVANTAGES AND ADVANTAGES

41

4 GOING WITH WOOD—HOW TO DO IT

47

5 WOOD GATHERING AND HARVESTING—TOOLS AND TIPS

59

6 FIREPLACES: THE ROMANTIC IN ALL OF US

65

7 WHAT GOES UP A CHIMNEY? SMOKE!

75

8 BUYING A WOOD-BURNING STOVE

87

9 THE WOOD-BURNER'S GLOSSARY

99

10 THE WOOD-BURNING STOVE CATALOG

103

Franklin Stoves   106
Scandinavian Stoves   118
Kitchen Cookstoves and Ranges   128
Box Stoves   134
Thermostatically Controlled Heaters   138
Other Wood Stoves   148
Fireplaces   156
Furnaces   163

APPENDIX

167

Where to Buy Wood-Burning Stoves   168

Characteristics of Woods for Fireplace Use   171

*Effects of Seasoning of Hardwoods on Moisture Content
and Heat Value   171*

Importance of Air-Dry Wood; Approximate Fuel Values   172

Ratings for Firewood   173

*Recommended Dimensions for Fireplaces and Size of
Flue Lining Required   173*

Heat Equivalents of Wood, By Species   174

Acknowledgments

It would not be possible to list the many, many people who gave so warmly and generously of their expertise, personal experiences, and time to the preparation of this book. Among those, however, to whom I am especially indebted are: David M. Barmgartner, Forest Resources Specialist, Cooperative Extension Service, Washington State University; Gary L. Bennett, Editor, CES, University of Maine; Einar Bergh, Deputy Director, Norwegian Information Service; William E. Dyer, Publisher, Alaska Highway News; John J. Garland, Timber Harvesting Specialist, CES, Oregon State University; John Guertler, the Historical Society of Pennsylvania; the Honorable Eero Korpivaara, Consulate General of Finland; Jens Krysel, Commercial Secretary, Consulate General of Denmark; Edward L. Palmer, Agricultural Engineer, CES, University of Connecticut; Mardis R. Warner, Agricultural Engineer, CES, University of Maine; Pierre Weill, the French embassy; F. E. Winch, Jr., Forester, CES, Cornell University; O. Lewis Wyman, State Program Coordinator, CES, University of Maine; John I. Zerbe, Director of Forest Products and Engineering Research, Forest Service, USDA; E. Douglas Cruickshank, Utilization & Marketing Forester, Forestry Department, Eastern Lane District, Springfield, Oregon.

In addition, my thanks for the tremendous amount of information and materials made available to me by USDA Extension Services and private organizations throughout the country, including: CES, University of Alaska; Finland National Tourist Office; Finnish Forestry Association, Forestry Information Service, Helsinki; National Forest Products Association; Research and Public Services, University of Maine; CES, Michigan State University; CES, University of New Hampshire; Forest Research Laboratory, School of Forestry, Oregon State University; Department of Forestry, University of Wisconsin.

And my very special thanks to my husband, Don, who took on the enormous task of finding, selecting, and preparing the illustrations that accompany the text.

Introduction

If you winced when you opened your last heating bill, you are probably one of the 50 million homeowners in the United States who are finding themselves faced with rapidly escalating heating costs. And it doesn't matter whether you heat with fuel oil, electricity, or gas—or a combination of fuels.

In January 1970 the cost of fuel oil in my area of Connecticut was 18.4¢ per gallon. Today it is 41.5¢. And my fuel oil company tells me it will probably be higher by my next delivery. There is also the problem of uncertain supply; over 40 percent of our fuel oil is imported from foreign countries with whom we have less than ideal relations. These supplies could be cut off at any time with a disastrous effect on our individual comfort, let alone our national economy.

My electric bills last summer were higher than they were the year before in the heart of the winter. People who have built or converted to all-electric homes on the electric company's assurance that it would be more economical than oil are gasping at bills of $200 a month for small homes. When I was in Ohio recently, I turned on the newscast for a weather check. One of the items in the news concerned a rise in electric rates for Medina. The electric company had complained that due to rising costs, its rate of profit was only about 6 percent; the company felt it was entitled to approximately 9 percent. The local officials thought this sounded reasonable, so the consumer was due to be hit with another rate increase. If I had to pay that electric bill, it wouldn't sound so reasonable to me. Especially if I had to switch from hamburger to spaghetti in order to pay it.

This reminds me of an incident I witnessed. An elderly, white-haired lady, neatly but shabbily dressed, was buying a few apples and two oranges in the market. As she counted out her money, she began to complain softly about the high cost of food. The cheerful vendor put an extra orange in her bag and said, "Don't worry as long as you have your health!" "Yes," responded his customer dourly, "and as long as I can pay my electric bill."

You're no better off with natural gas. Price controls may be lifted at any time; meanwhile, serious shortages are predicted in many areas. There is no shortage of it worldwide; there are simply no plans for delivering it where it is wanted.

At the receiving end of all these price increases, shortages, and profitable investments is the consumer—with no one to pass his increased costs on to, no one to protect his investments, if he still has any.

Is there any alternative? There is. You don't have to take it lying down. You can join the thousands of cosy, happy homeowners who have bought a wood-burning stove.

I recently interviewed a young woman who, with her daughter, lives in a large, modern house in nearby Redding. She has just installed two Lange stoves to heat 6,000 cubic feet. Three years ago, in a house in Weston, an ice storm deprived her of electricity for ten days and ten nights; not only was she without heat, means for cooking, and water, she had to put her dog in a kennel and lost $3,000 worth of rare plants. "That's a stupid situation to be in when you can have a wood stove," she said. She has had wood stoves ever since. She has a new collection of plants, and she confidently looks forward to a cosy winter—burning chunk wood and logs. "I won't lose a single plant," she assured me.

"Won't you supplement your heat with your central heating system?" I asked.

"The furnace for this area is cracked," she answered with a grin. "But I won't need it. I've used wood-burning stoves ever since the ice storm—and before that in Maine near the Canadian border. We'll be comfortable and we won't be at the mercy of the weather and the electric company."

The dealer who sold her the stoves came to her house to measure and make recommendations. With 6,000 cubic feet to heat—including twelve-foot ceilings and glass walls—they advised her *against* installing the largest Lange available. "You don't need it," they assured her. "These two medium-sized models will do the job."

Wood is a traditional source of fuel for cooking and heating. Our country was colonized, grew and prospered on wood. Wood fueled industry and transportation and built our cities. When the use of wood began to decline— in the late 1800s—it was due not to a shortage of wood, but to the availability and easier handling characteristics of coal; later, gas, electricity, and fuel oil continued the movement away from wood. These are no longer viable alternatives. They are pricing themselves out of the market; they come from supplies that will be exhausted in the foreseeable future; and they are polluting the earth.

Wood is nonpolluting and beautiful. It can be grown and harvested like

Large stove in a modern home in Redding, Connecticut. Fire has just been lit and door is about to be closed. Photo by Marj Loeper.

any other crop, a completely renewable resource. Instead of land made ugly and uninhabitable by strip-mining and oil derricks, we can have glorious forests teeming with birds and wildlife. Instead of oil spills, we can return the oceans to the creatures that live in them, and we can once again glean an edible harvest from the sea.

With wood as fuel we can clean up our air so that it is fit to breathe instead of "unsatisfactory." We can once again discover family life built around a home with a wood-burning stove, perhaps a fireplace for pure pleasure, and even a large, lovely cast-iron kitchen cookstove complete with stew pot and the smell of good baking.

Let's not just talk about the good old days—let's bring the best of them back with a wood-burning stove.

Vintage potbellied stove in use today in the Alpha-Bit, a popular shop for crafts, books, soup and sandwiches in Mapleton, Oregon. Photo courtesy of Oregon Forestry Department, Eastern Lane District.

the Wood-Burning Stove Book

1. From the Cave to the Colonies

Along with food and shelter, warmth has been essential to man's existence in most parts of the earth, and to starve from want of fire was nearly as desperate a state as to starve from want of food.

Victorian children were tearfully regaled with the heartrending story of the little match girl who froze to death when her meager supply of matches was exhausted, and only recently an elderly upstate New York couple died of the cold when their utilities were turned off because they could not pay their bill. The farmer with his back woodlot is in a much more fortunate position today than the city dweller with his complete dependence on public utilities. Perhaps one day warmth will be considered as much of a right as food and we will have heat stamps as well as food stamps for the truly needy.

The important place that fire has always held in man's esteem is shown by the fact that almost all early religions—from the very primitive to the more-developed beliefs of the Greeks and Romans—incorporated a legend to account for the gift of fire to man. In Greek and Roman mythology, fire was the celestial gift of Prometheus, who stole it from the gods and bore it to earth. In their anger, the gods doomed him to a terrible and eternal punishment.

Since the origin of fire goes back to prehistory, we can only surmise how man actually discovered it. Possibly early man captured fire from a blaze started by lightning or by lava overflowing a volcano; Stone Age man might have discovered it while working flints to make weapons—a spark falling among dry grass could have been his first experience.

Whatever the source, fire was a "civilizing" influence and is credited with the development of the home. A hunter, instead of tearing apart his kill in the woods or prairie, proudly carried the meat home to be delectably cooked over the campfire in front of his own cave. Later, probably tiring of rebuilding fires after rains, he moved the fire indoors to his cave living room. We have found the remains of many cave fires with large numbers of bones; archeologists argue about whether the bones were left from food prepared over the fire or were used as fuel. With my use-everything-twice approach to daily living, I don't see these ideas as mutually exclusive; conceivably the bones may have been gnawed at until they were bare of meat, then set aside for burning—but perhaps it's more complicated than that.

A cave fire sounds like a smoky sort of heat until we realize that many caves have cracks and openings in their roofs and walls that lead to the outside. Choosing a good cave may have included a knowledge of drafts as well as other factors, and some caves undoubtedly had excellent natural draft systems. In addition, the stone walls of the cave reflected and retained the heat in a way our modern frame buildings and upholstered living rooms do not. The tendency to think of primitive man as living in great discomfort may be far from the fact; in this, as in so many areas, we may be priding ourselves on nonexistent advances over the past.

Man-built shelters, developed with the advance of civilization, lacked

A caricature of King George III toasting muffins. From an etching by James Gillray, 1791.

many of the amenities of the cave. A castle was a very drafty, uncomfortable place with poor sanitary facilities and cold food brought at great distance from the enormous kitchens in which it was prepared.

The castle was heated by huge fires, originally built in the center of the great high-ceilinged halls, which drew all the heat to the ceiling and left the stone floor untouched by warmth. Eventually the fire was moved to one wall and a simple straight chimney was added. Although this got rid of some of the smoke, it was not much help in heating, since a large fireplace—and castle fireplaces were large enough to stand in—provides heat only when a large fire burns fiercely in it. When the fire burns down, the inside corners of the fireplace become cold, and hot air is drawn out of the room allowing fresh air to rush in. As with modern houses, castles were more often cooled than heated by their fireplaces.

It took many centuries for Europeans to discover that a small fireplace with a small, steadily burning fire would provide more heat than a large one, which ate up wood while providing very little and very uneven warmth.

Some of this discomfort was due to a curious historical phenomenon; knowledge is discovered, used, and lost over and over again. The Romans, who were excellent engineers—as we know from their roads and aqueducts, which still stand today—developed heating systems under their tiled floors that were very modern both in concept and in execution. With the fall of Rome, this simple invention, which contributed so much to comfortable living, was lost and was not discovered again until scholars excavated Roman sites.

By colonial times heating had once again become sophisticated; the Dutch, German, Scandinavian, and French heating units were impressively efficient and satisfactory. The English, however, stubbornly stuck to the open fireplace of which they were so fond, and froze in their frame houses from Vermont to Virginia. Eventually, thanks to Ben Franklin and Count Rumford, fireplaces became smaller—and developed smoke shelves, dampers, and other useful devices. The exception was the kitchen fireplace, which remained large because of its function; cooking was done over the open fire, to one side of the fire on coals raked from the fire proper, and in ovens set within and without the fireplace as well as in front of it. Many kitchen fireplaces contained cosy corners in which one could sit and warm himself, and herbs and vegetables were hung to dry on the wall above the lintel.

As cities grew and forests receded, it became more difficult and expensive to feed the enormous appetite of inefficient colonial fireplaces. By the middle of the eighteenth century there was a real shortage of wood in Philadelphia, and Ben Franklin set his inventive genius to the problem. The result was "The Pennsylvanian Fire-place," which he invented in 1744 and described in a published account, complete with diagrams, measurements, and instructions for building and installing.

A caricature of Queen Charlotte frying sprats. From an etching by James Gillray, 1791.

THE FIRST FRANKLIN FIRE-PLACE

The "New-Invented Pennsylvanian Fire-place" was designed—of course—to allow viewing of the open fire, but to do so while burning wood more efficiently than in a regular fireplace. With his new fire-place Franklin noted: "my common Room, I know, is twice as warm as it used to be, with a quarter of the wood formerly consumed there."

So that it might render maximum efficiency, he even described how to use it:

Your cord wood must be cut into three lengths; or else a short piece, fit for the fire-place, cut off, and the longer left for the kitchen or other fires. Dry hickory or ash, or any woods that burn with a clear flame, are rather to be chosen, because such are less apt to foul the smoke passages with soot; and flame communicates with its light, as well as by contact, greater heat to the plates and room.

Made of cast iron, the stove was designed to fit into an existing fireplace. It was an open box, joined together with screws and mortared to seal the seams. The front opening was fitted with a solid iron plate, or "shutter," which could be moved up and down to create or control draft while tending the fire, or closed completely when no fire was wanted. The floor of the box curved up in front "to keep coals and ashes from coming to the floor."

Although it looks simple at first glance, the construction was fairly complicated. A false back of from two to four inches was constructed so that "no air may pass into the chimney but what goes under the false back, and up behind it." This, to some extent, cut down on drafts, since no air was drawn into the chimney except through the fire.

Franklin further increased the efficiency of the device by using it to heat additional air. "A passage is made, communicating with the outward air, to introduce air into the fore part of the hollow under the bottom plate, whence it may rise through an air-hole into the air-box." In other words, a channel was made to the outdoors, from front to back, underneath the firebox. The air was thus brought into a shaft that rose directly in back of the fire, and was released into the room through an opening at the top of a baffled shaft, at which point it had been thoroughly heated.

In addition, Dr. Franklin got more mileage out of the smoke and air rising from the fire; he channeled it up and around the shaft, forcing it to seek the chimney by going down a channel in back of the shaft, then up into a space beneath the fire-place floor, and finally up the chimney. By forcing it to travel so much farther before it reached the chimney, he burned the smoke and gases more completely than was possible with an open fire; more heat remained in the fire-place—and thus available to the room—than formerly.

Nor did Franklin neglect the small niceties, such as the comfort of the nonsmoker in what he visualized as a fairly draft-free room. "In rooms where much smoking of tobacco is used, it is also convenient to have a small hole, about five or six inches square, cut near the ceiling through into the funnel; this hole must have a shutter, by which it may be closed or opened at pleasure. When open, there will be strong draft of air through it into the chimney, which will presently carry off a cloud of smoke, and keep the room clear."

It is not immediately obvious in looking at the illustrations of the Pennsyl-

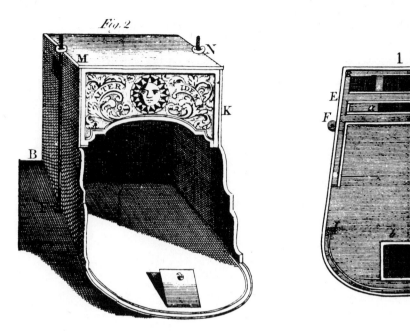

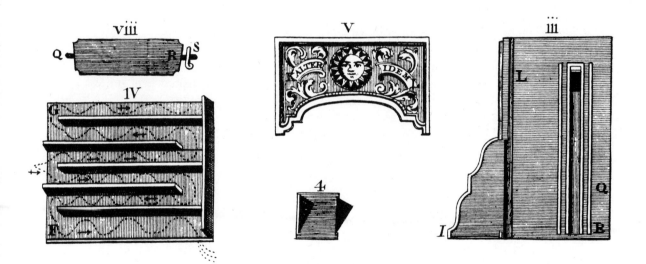

Franklin's drawings for his Pennsylvanian Fire-place, Fig. 2. Front of stove; I. Bottom plate; VIII. Shutter; IV. One of two middle plates in air passage behind fire; V. Ornamented front plate; III. Side plate, showing channels to accept the two middle plates which form the air passage.

vanian fire-place, but it was meant to be used with andirons; they created a better draft and, therefore, a hotter fire. The fireplace itself required the same sort of upkeep as any cast-iron stove: it needed to be treated against rust. Franklin suggested the use of "powder of black lead" mixed with a little rum and water: "as it dries, rub it to a gloss with the same brush, so the joints will not be discerned, but it will look all of a piece, and shine like new iron."

The Franklin fire-place proved immensely popular and was soon being manufactured throughout the colonies. Since Franklin did not believe in patents, he placed no restriction on his inventions, and the Franklin stove was soon being manufactured both to his design and with alterations of which he did not approve. His name was used freely, as it is today, to adorn stoves far removed from the principles on which his original fireplace stove was based. In 1769, disturbed by the misuse of his invention, he wrote:

Soon after the foregoing piece was published, some persons in England, in imitation of Mr. Franklin's invention, made what they called "Pennsylvanian Fire-places, with Improvements"; the principal of which pretended improvements is, a contraction of the passages in the air-box, originally designed for admitting a quantity of fresh air, and warning it as it entered the room. The contracting these passages gains indeed more room for the grate, but in a great measure defeats their intention. For, if the passages in the air-box do not greatly exceed in dimensions the amount of all the crevices by which cold air can enter the room, they will not considerably prevent, as they were intended to do, the entry of cold air through these crevices.

The first Franklin stove of that name was patented in 1816 and subsequent patents were issued for Slide-Door Franklin Stoves, Closed Franklin Stoves, Pipe Franklin Stoves, and Fold-Door Franklin Stoves, among others. It was soon found that the stove, whatever its variation in design, would heat more effectively if installed outside—rather than within—the fireplace, with a pipe leading to the fireplace chimney. This variation is found to this day, although there are also modern Franklin stoves that still nestle within the fireplace proper.

THE SECOND FRANKLIN—FIRST OF THE DOWNDRAFT STOVES

By 1786 Franklin had lived abroad for some years and become acquainted with European heating devices. Although he never lost his love of an open wood fire, he reluctantly came to the conclusion that it was not the most efficient method of heating. However, none of the existing heating devices met with his complete approval, and he set about devising one that would be more satisfactory. The result was described in considerable detail in a paper entitled: "Description of a new Stove for burning Pitcoal, and consuming all its Smoke," which was presented to the American Philosophical Society on January 28, 1786. Although described as a stove for pitcoal, it was equally suitable for burning wood, and Franklin's directions cover both fuels.

The new stove's appearance was most unexpected and unusual, although strictly functional. It looked like a vase set on two boxes, the larger one on the floor. with a smaller one on top, then the vase, complete with a brass flame-shaped finial.

As Franklin described it:

Its principle is that of a siphon reversed, operating on air in a manner somewhat similar to the operation of the common siphon on water. The funnel of the chimney is the longer leg, the vase is the shorter; and as, in the common siphon, the weight of water in the longer leg is greater than that in the shorter leg; and thus in descending permits the water in the shorter leg to rise, by the pressure of the atmosphere; so in this aerial siphon, the levity of the air in the longer leg being greater than that in the shorter, it rises and permits the pressure of the atmosphere to force that in the shorter to descend. This causes the smoke to descend, also, and in passing through the burning coals it is kindled into flame, thereby heating more the passages in the iron box whereon the vase which contains the coals is placed; and retarding at the same time the consumption of the coals.

Like the first Pennsylvania fire-place, it was designed to keep smoke and volatiles as long as possible within the stove; in addition, it assured more complete combustion by forcing the smoke down through the fire. In other words, it was a true downdraft construction.

After describing in detail the parts of the stove, complete with dimensions, and telling exactly how to "fix this machine," Dr. Franklin goes on to explain how to use it.

Let the first fire be made after eight in the evening, or before eight in the morning, for at those times and between those hours all night, there is usually a draft up a chimney, though it has long been without fire; but between those hours in the day there is often, in a cold chimney, a draft downwards, when, if you attempt to kindle a fire, the smoke will come into the room.

And in case this wasn't entirely clear, he took further precautions:

But to be certain of your proper time, hold a flame over the air-hole at the top. If the flame is drawn strongly down for a continuance, without whiffling, you may begin to kindle a fire.

Having determined the draft is in your favor, the fire may be laid and lit. The vase was constructed so that air entered through the flame finial, was drawn down through the burning wood into the ash box, where it traversed through winding passages, and finally made its way up the chimney. In Franklin's view:

The effect of this machine, well managed, is to burn not only the coals, but all the smoke of the coals, so that while the fire is burning, if you go out and observe the top of your chimney, you will see no smoke issuing, nor any thing but clear warm air, which as usual makes the bodies seen through it appear waving.

He further stressed the advantages of his new invention:

The air heated over common fires instantly quits the room and goes up the chimney with the smoke; but in the stove, it is obliged to descend in flame and pass through the long winding horizontal passages, communicating its heat to a body of iron plate, which, having thus time to receive the heat, communicates the same to the air of the room, and thereby warms it to a greater degree.

The whole of the fuel is consumed by being turned into flame, and you have the benefit of its heat.

Unfortunately, while apparently logical in principle, the stove worked less perfectly when put to actual use. It was difficult to operate and required a great deal of loving attention. Even Franklin admitted that it could not be left to the occasional ministrations of servants but had to be tended by someone working in the same room and able to keep an eye on it. Subsequent efforts to create downdraft stoves have encountered similar problems—especially back-puffing; today many so-called downdraft stoves lead the air across rather than down through the fire.

GERMAN AND HOLLAND STOVES

Most colonial stoves were made of cast iron, a stove material which goes back at least as far as A.D. 25—the date of the earliest cast-iron stove of which we have an example. This was a Chinese stove, cast in one piece rather than in plates.

The earliest records we have of cast-iron stoves in Europe date them around the end of the fifteenth century, when they began to assume their present form. They were built with rectangular plates and the number of plates gave the stove its basic designation, five-plate stove, ten-plate stove, and so on.

The five-plate stoves were the ones first used by German colonists in Pennsylvania. They had five sides and were open at one end. The open end projected either into the outdoors, or at a later period, into a room known as the stove room. In the latter, the wood was brought in from outdoors, conveniently stacked in the room, and fed into the stove as needed. The closed rear of the stove projected into the room it was to heat and rested on legs or on a platform. Sometimes the open front end of the stove rested on a hearth for easy filling. The stove room was never used for any other purpose—although I suspect it functioned somewhat like our modern "mud" rooms, holding wet boots and outdoor clothing.

Aside from its efficiency in heating surprisingly large areas, the stove had a big advantage in that there were no openings in the heated room and, therefore, no way for smoke to get into the room. It was also impossible, however, to look at the fire to judge whether or not more wood was needed without going into the other room.

Occasionally, instead of being relegated to a separate room, the stove opened into a working fireplace, the kitchen fireplace, for instance. This allowed the stove to be fired with hot coals and burning wood from an already well burning fire; it heated the stove up quickly, and only one fire needed to be built for both cooking (in the fireplace) and heating (in the stove). The Germans and Dutch did not attempt to heat themselves with the fireplace, but like the English colonists, they still required it for cooking.

Examples of these colonial stoves can be seen in many museums and historical societies around the country. They were sometimes known as jamb stoves and were decorated most pleasingly with raised patterns illustrating Biblical subjects, with descriptions or titles in German. As in today's Scandinavian stoves, the decorations were utilitarian as well as attractive; they strengthened the plates and increased the area of the surface from which heat was radiated. These early stoves were sand-cast, and some modern stoves are still manufactured by this painstaking method.

The Dutch, or Holland, stoves were mostly six-plate stoves and had a door opening into the room in which they stood—rather than an opening into the stove room. They were set away from the wall or fireplace and connected to a flue by a pipe. Franklin defended his failure to use them instead of his Pennsylvanian fire-place:

> The Holland iron stove . . . its conveniences are, that it makes a room all over warm; for the chimney being wholly closed except the flue of the stove, very little air is required to supply that, and therefore not much rushes in at crevices, or at the door when it is opened. Little fuel serves, the heat being almost all saved; for it rays out almost equally from the four sides, the bottom, and the top, into the room, and presently warms the air around it, which being rarified, rises to the ceiling, and its place is supplied by the lower air of the room, which flows gradually towards the stove, and is there warmed and rises in its turn, so that there is a continual circulation till all the air in the room is warmed. . . . But they have these inconveniences. There is no sight of the fire, which is in itself a pleasant thing. One cannot conveniently make any other use of the fire but that of warming the room.

Considering how cold it got in the colonies, one would think that merely warming the room would be sufficient, but Franklin resolutely turned away from these excellent stoves and continued to struggle with his inventions. He is no doubt vindicated by the fact that even today Franklin stoves have a place on the market, and the consumer will often turn away from the airtight box stoves to buy a stove that allows him to view the open fire.

SOAPSTONE STOVES

This is a peculiarly American type of stove, which was first manufactured in 1797. It was made from native soapstone quarried in New Hampshire, Vermont, and Massachusetts. As anyone knows who has ever cooked with a soapstone griddle, it is unequaled for the length of time it holds heat—once it is thoroughly heated. In that respect, it resembles the famous Scandinavian tile stoves (which are not, so far as I know, imported into this country). Today soapstone stoves are in short supply, but they are still made, I believe, by at least one manufacturer in Vermont, who also makes other objects, such as griddles, out of soapstone.

AIRTIGHT STOVES

The first airtight stoves were made of so-called Russia sheet iron. They were oval rather than rectangular and had a door with a draft in it as well as a hinged top opening through which large chunks of wood were placed on the fire.

Their invention is attributed to Isaac Orr of Washington, D.C., who introduced them in the early nineteenth century; by the middle of the century these stoves included self-regulating draft systems—their basic design has not changed much to this day. They were considered an appreciable advance over other stove designs and were readily converted to coal, which became the heating fuel for Victorians—although they still retained their love of fireplaces and built them into their handsome homes.

THE KITCHEN RANGE

Stove design probably reached its peak in the kitchen range. Once the effectiveness of stoves for home heating was fully appreciated, designers turned to the kitchen fireplace and saw that it was an arduous and primitive way of cooking. Many flat-topped stoves had already been pressed into service for teakettles and other small cooking chores, but it was not until the nineteenth century that the immense kitchen range took over all the functions of heating, cooking, baking, and laundry. The best and most elaborate kitchen ranges did just about everything: they had a large reservoir that kept hot water always available; they had ovens for baking, whose products have never been surpassed by modern stoves; they kept the soup pot simmering on the back of the stove while griddle cakes fried in front and herbs dried in the warming oven, which also kept plates hot for dinner service. There was even a low rim which stood invitingly at just the right height for toasting one's toes or drying wet socks. Chicks incubated happily, and the kitchen cat curled itself up in

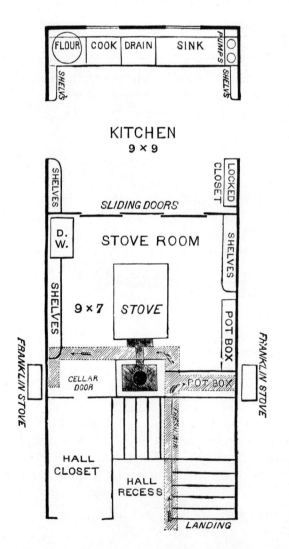

Floor plan showing kitchen and stove room in nineteenth-century home, in which "the chimney and stove room are contrived to ventilate the whole house." From The Housekeeper's Manual *by Catherine E. Beecher and Harriet Beecher Stowe, 1873, New York.*

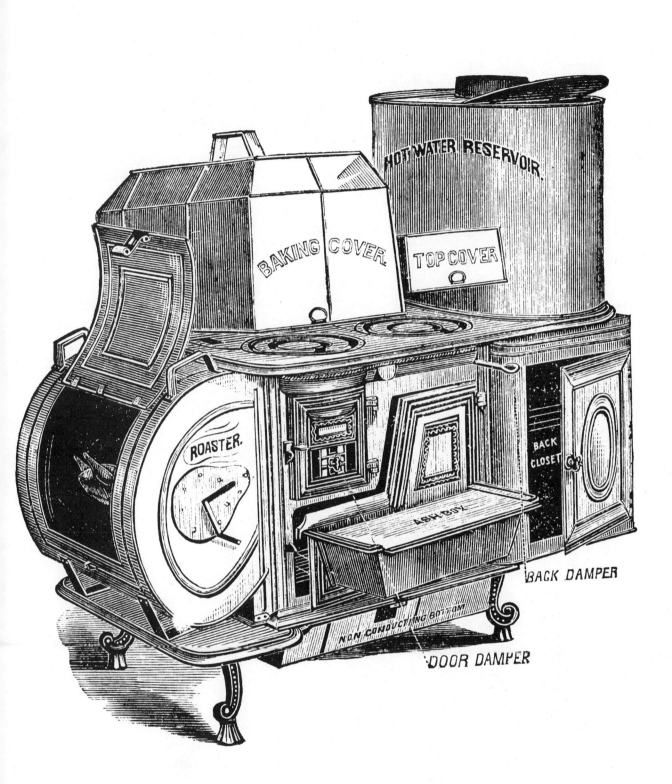

"A cooking-stove constructed on true scientific principles." From The Housekeeper's Manual *by Catherine E. Beecher and Harriet Beecher Stowe, 1873, New York.*

appropriate spots on the stove. It became the great, black, pulsating heart of the house—to live on in the memory of anyone who has ever experienced it.

Nothing awakens nostalgia or elicits more stories than a question to someone who has known a kitchen range in childhood. Coming from an icy bedroom to the warmth and fragrance of the kitchen is bound to induce a feeling of gratitude and pleasure, and it is no wonder that the countrywoman is so often pictured in rosy-cheeked, aproned bustle as she takes a pan of fresh-baked blueberry muffins from the oven and stirs the oatmeal that has been in the making since the night before.

Antique kitchen ranges are in great demand and command high prices, despite the fact that they are cast iron and must be blackened regularly—or they will rust in the humidity of steaming kettles and soup pots and rainy summer days. If you have your heart set on the old type of cookstove, however, check your dimensions; they were very large and not many kitchens have the room for them plus the necessary woodbox and ash bucket.

OTHER WOOD-BURNING STOVES

In their heyday wood-burning stoves heated Mississippi riverboats, ran steam locomotives, powered factories, and were used to heat large public buildings. Furnaces were common and very effective, providing they were sufficiently close to a source of supply. Today there are still factories in the United States heated by wood-burning furnaces, although many of them use sawdust or bark—excellent sources of high-quality heat. Wood-burning furnaces of smaller dimension and less awesome fuel requirements are practical for home use, and there is even a furnace which can use fuel oil and wood alternately —depending on your requirements and the state of your budget.

STOVE CATEGORIES

In a way, all stove categories are arbitrary and confusing, because often a stove appears under more than one category. For instance, sometimes a stove is described by the way it functions: airtight, Franklin, downdraft, thermostatic; sometimes for where it is used: parlor stoves, four o'clock stoves, kitchen stoves; and sometimes just for the way it looks: potbelly stoves, box stoves, illuminated stoves, and gallery stoves.

In addition, stoves are thought of in terms of the materials of which they are constructed: cast iron, Russia sheet iron, soapstone, firebrick and ceramic, and so on. Since stoves were superseded as heating devices by the advent of central heating and the use of coal, fuel oil, and gas, stove designs have not changed much since the nineteenth century. It is surprising, given these circumstances, that so many well-constructed and well-designed stoves

Antique French stove from the collection of De Dietrich & Cie. Photo courtesy of Pierre Weill, French Embassy.

are available today; it is not surprising that no spectacular new changes have been made in the stoves our grandfathers knew. It may be that stove technology is as advanced as it can be; but if you turn to wood burning, keep in mind that perhaps you may be the one to have the insight and inventiveness to develop some new and simple device—like the smoke shelf, the damper, or the baffle—for which a chilly world will thank you in generations to come. It's one sure way of having your name go down in history.

American Drawing Room or Parlor Stove. Art Journal Catalogue of Crystal Palace Exhibition, London, 1851.

2. Wood–the Ecologist's Fuel

Today almost everyone is aware of two major problems confronting life as we know it in the United States: pollution and the shortage of the fossil fuels, oil and coal. Actually neither of the fossil fuels is presently in short supply, although it is estimated that fuel oil supplies will be exhausted in thirty-five years unless new deposits are discovered. At the moment there is plenty of oil, but we have to import 40 percent of it at increasingly prohibitive prices from other countries; there is plenty of coal, but mining it is both costly and ecologically harmful. Even the consumer who is unconcerned about ecology takes notice when his pocketbook is affected; the price of these fuels has risen to the point where everyone is hurting. Electricity, used as a substitute for fossil fuels, is manufactured in large part by the use of them, and it is even more costly than they are.

As the cost of common heating and cooking fuels continues to rise—and it will continue to rise—many people are searching for alternatives. While there is a limit to how far the thermostat can be turned down without actual hardship resulting, there is apparently no limit to the extent to which inflationary costs can be passed on by public utilities and private fuel oil companies to the consumer. We are on a collision course. The intelligent consumer looks around, sees what is coming, and makes plans for the future. Fortunately, the solution is near at hand; it is economical, feasible, and a pleasant improvement in life-style—it is the substitution of wood for other heating and cooking fuels.

A wood stove is both ecologically sound and economically within the range of everyone. It is a psychological comfort, fulfillment, and delight. It comforts in its gentle warmth; it gives the satisfaction of personal achievement, because you are being heated by your own efforts; it is a delight because it brings the consumer into intimate contact with nature and with one of nature's most fascinating and beautiful things—a wood fire.

The use of wood as fuel, however, inevitably raises certain questions. The one most often asked is: "Wouldn't a return to wood as fuel decimate our forests?"

WOOD AS A RENEWABLE RESOURCE

Most people who have lived on a piece of country property for more than ten years have seen with their own eyes how the forest renews itself. In our small part of Fairfield County, we wage a constant battle with black locust trees. The summer lawn is usually cut once a week; sometimes other chores press closely and this schedule is neglected. If the lawn goes two weeks without cutting, it is not only shaggy, it is also liberally spiked with foot-high black locust seedlings. Turn your back for a month and the seedlings have grown

Exterior of typical sauna in Finland.
A small, wood-heated structure built
by the water's edge to "facilitate
customary dip after steaming." Photo
courtesy of Finnish Travel Information
Bureau.

too large to cut comfortably with hand clippers. If you painstakingly cut down young trees in the meadow that have sprung up unobserved, you find a host of small seedlings sprouting in no time at all from the miniature stump and from an area four to six feet in diameter. We had several trees downed by an ice storm a few years ago; today one of the most tedious chores on the grounds is cutting back the shoots, which still come up from the stumps and the wide-spreading roots close to the surface. It is endless. Yet if we didn't persist, each one of those shoots would grow in record time to a seventy-five-foot giant.

Our land abuts some twenty or thirty acres of thick woods that have been left in a wild state for over sixty years. An elderly resident of ninety-two recalls the days when he used to pasture his small herd of cows on that very land. "There weren't many trees then," he told me, "only meadow. In fact we set up a bit of a golf course. Where those woods are—it was all grass and buttercups in those days."

Walking through the dense stands of sugar maple, beech, and various hickories, it is hard to imagine the land as he knew it then. I would expect

Finnish boys, inside sauna, sprinkling water on wood-burning stove. Photo courtesy of Consulate General of Finland.

from my own experience that today it would be solid black locust and poison ivy, but nature manages things better than we might think.

The return to the woods of this small bit of land is not an isolated instance. Finland, a tiny country of extensive forests, has for centuries been a large exporter of wood products; much of the world's supply of newsprint, plywood, and other wood-based items comes from Finland. Yet today Finland has greater and more productive forests than it had forty years ago.

Finland's increased productivity is due entirely to good forest management. In 1922 Finland had 25.3 million hectares of forests; in 1938, 24.8 million; in 1963, 21.7 million; and in the beginning of 1965—the latest figures available from the consulate general's office in New York—22.1 million. This, in spite of the fact that Finland's forest area is now almost 13 percent smaller than it was thirty-five years ago, due to territorial concessions made after World War II. Nor is Finland resting on its laurels. Although forest lands in Finland are 63 percent privately owned, private ownership in cooperation with government programs and research is confidently looking forward to a future of even greater productivity.

Europe, densely populated and highly industrialized, came late to forest management; today European forests are growing, rather than diminishing, in both extent and productivity. Germany's famous and ancient Black Forest has been harvested for over 600 years; visitors to the Black Forest today see woods more productive and just as beautiful as in the centuries before man's invasion of them.

In every case where wood has proven an economically desirable product, forest productivity has been increased. Man has the technology to harness nature to his needs in the production of wood as well as in the production of less ecologically desirable products.

Since our immediate concern, however, is with the forest resources of the United States, what is the situation here?

When the pioneers began to clear land in the New World for their homes, farms, and cities, they marveled at the apparently endless forests. By the eighteenth century, Ben Franklin was turning his inventive skills to a stove that would help ease the shortage of wood around Philadelphia. Today, two centuries later, the United States still has almost 75 percent as much forest land as existed in the time of the pioneers—754 million acres, or one third of the United States, is still forest. Of that acreage, 254 million acres have been set apart for parks and recreation areas and cannot be commercially cut for lumber, but they are still available to those gathering wood by permit. The remaining 500 million acres are classified as commercial forest land—forest land which may be harvested. In the state of Maine, for example, 90 percent of the land is forest—admittedly, more than in any other state—but Maine is also the site of some of the largest paper manufacturers in the country, and 86 percent of the forest land is commercial acreage.

From our commercial forest land comes all of our plywood, paper, wood pulp, building lumber, and other wood products—supporting some of the largest and most essential industries in the country; yet even today we are growing more wood than we are harvesting. This is due largely to good forest management by industrial users.

It may seem strange that the greatest increase in wood production lies in the most commercially active areas, but because the wood is a money crop, forest land that is used for harvesting is more wisely managed and more productive than forest land that is allowed to grow untended. Just as a vegetable garden, cultivated intensively, can produce greater quantities of food than those same plants growing wild in a meadow, so a managed forest plantation is more productive than a wild forest. Once wood is as important to a homeowner as his vegetable garden, wood production can be stepped up, and productivity, it is estimated, can be at least doubled.

WOOD HARVESTING AND THE QUALITY OF FORESTS

The question then arises—does intensive production and harvesting of forests deplete the land and decrease the quality of the forest? Happily the answer is—on the contrary.

A well-managed forest produces more young trees, healthier older trees; it eliminates diseased, crooked, and crowded trees. Older trees consume as much or more oxygen than they create; an average acre of healthy young trees gives off four tons of oxygen and consumes five to six tons of carbon monoxide a year. Not only does it not create pollution, it actually acts as an antipollution device to a much greater extent than an unmanaged forest. In addition, as anyone knows who has walked in a forest on a hot day or planted a shade tree to cool the living room, forests are natural air conditioners; and a managed forest is a better air conditioner than an unmanaged one because young trees are more efficient in this respect than older trees, whose photosynthesis goes mostly to maintaining their own existence. A young tree has a cooling effect equivalent to ten room-sized air conditioners running twenty hours a day. Since air conditioners use tremendous amounts of electricity, some thought might be given by the beleaguered householder to planting a tree—even if he doesn't mean to burn wood.

In addition, trees are humidifiers; they release moisture through leaves and needles into the atmosphere, and it is estimated that the combined cooling and humidifying created by a forest is equal to that created by the same area of ocean.

But what of wildlife? Nature practices forest management with fires, hurricanes, disease, and other catastrophes; although she achieves the desired effect, nature is wasteful. She can afford to be because she is merely maintaining a balance and is not concerned with harvest. Man can approximate the same conditions but less wastefully and more efficiently without disturbing the natural balance of the forest.

Wildlife requires a certain amount of underbrush, new young trees, meadow, and sunlight. A deep forest canopy leaves no food for deer or quail and actually discourages wildlife. In managed national forests the deer population has increased by as much as 500 percent since 1920, and by 800 percent in the South (according to the Department of Interior's Bureau of Sport Fisheries and Wildlife). Ruffed grouse, turkey, and other once-declining wild creatures have made similar gains. Man has studied and imitated natural ways of forest management; forest fires are now sometimes started deliberately and allowed to burn under controlled conditions, because it has been shown that some trees and vegetation benefit from fire more than from other methods of management.

When I first learned of this, I was startled at the thought of fire being used as a forest management tool; but I remembered how the farmers in the neck of the woods where I grew up used to get together on a dry early spring day to burn off the meadows so that the blueberry bushes would give their best yield. It was always an occasion for picnics and lots of lemonade—guarding the perimeters of the fire with a broom and keeping a sharp eye on it as it spread in an ever-widening ring from the center of the meadow was hot work. The crop of blueberries in midsummer was well worth it.

In other words, forest management does not fight nature; it tries to learn from her and to imitate her just as the vegetable gardener does. The result, as we see in other countries as well as in our own, is bigger, better, and healthier forests that we can harvest as we do a vegetable garden, actually improving rather than destroying our natural resources.

As the Forest Service of the USDA wrote me when I asked whether they considered wood a renewable resource:

Wood is indeed a renewable resource and the production of wood on a sustained yield basis may be enhanced by various approaches which include: (1) improving the sites through fertilization, drainage, and irrigation; (2) converting forest areas to faster-growing species; (3) improving stocking and shortening the rotation through reforestation; (4) introducing genetically faster-growing trees; (5) stimulating the growth of the desired species through seeding; (6) recovering a larger share of the gross forest production through thinnings; and (7) reducing losses from fire, insects, and diseases through better forest protection.

And lest you may think that faster-growing trees mean increasing production of softwoods, let me tell you that my black locusts, which grow faster than the fastest weeds in my lawn, are rated—along with shagbark hickory— as one of the highest heat-producing hardwoods in America.

WOOD-BURNING AND AIR POLLUTION

In talking with people about the advisability of burning wood instead of other fuels, I have most often been asked about the polluting quality of wood smoke and other volatiles as compared to the volatiles of fuel oil and coal.

In the first place, there is one interesting fact about the chemistry of wood-burning; the carbon dioxide that is released by burning is not different in quantity or content from that released by that same wood decaying on the forest floor. In that sense, any pollutants from wood may be said to be "natural," in that they occur in nature and, therefore, may be assumed not to be harmful to the environment. In contrast, fossil fuels when burned give off large quantities of sulfur dioxide—a volatile not normally found in the atmosphere. Since sulfur dioxide is the substance that is causing statues and buildings that have stood for thousands of years to literally crumble to dust, it is obviously not a very good substance to be breathing into our much less adamant lungs. Nature has its own way of dealing with its own pollutants so that they do not interfere with the health and growth of her plants and animals; she has not been able to cope equally well with man-made pollutants, and so far, neither has man himself.

In the second place, wood properly burned to complete combustion releases far fewer volatiles into the atmosphere than wood incompletely burned. There is no reason why wood should not be completely burned; with the availability of well-designed stoves and a little common sense, most combustion can take place under ideal conditions.

WOOD AS A SOLAR FUEL

Another reason wood is the favored fuel of ecologists is that it can be classed as "solar" fuel.

The very elements that wood gives off when burned, carbon dioxide, moisture, and energy, are the elements it converts from the atmosphere when growing; on the average, trees convert these three elements into wood fiber at the rate of four tons per acre. The energy, which we receive as wood heat, is solar energy—free for the taking and never depleted.

Other fuels, coal, oil, and electricity, require pollution-creating devices to make them useful; wood aids the environment at the same time that it is creating fuel. It is the only fuel that is completely clean while it is being prepared for burning. The greatest pollution wood creates is in the use of the chain saw or log splitter—and if necessary, even these small aids could be eliminated in favor of hand-driven saws and machines.

Wood is even cleaner as fuel than most so-called solar heating. As presently constituted, most solar heating devices depend heavily on plastics, which are environmentally harmful to manufacture and environmentally harmful to dispose of since they are not biodegradable. This is not to say that solar heating is not a great improvement over the use of fossil fuels; but at present it is too expensive for the average consumer, must be accompanied by supplemental heat sources in the very areas where heat is most needed for longest periods, and requires elaborate new construction or expensive changes in existing buildings. It also dictates an architecture of its own which is not pleasing aesthetically to many people.

SUMMARY

All things considered, there is no question that wood is the most desirable fuel in terms of ecology. Its use would improve rather than adversely affect our environment, and until something better comes along, it is by far the least expensive solution to rising fuel costs. If wood fuel becomes popular, it will, of course, become just as expensive as everything else. It is up to every consumer, both as an individual and as part of the government, to see that costs are kept reasonable and realistic, and that increased demand does not lead to increased profits in an area so closely related to the public interest.

3. Heating with Wood–Disadvantages and Advantages

Most of us have never had to fend for ourselves in a physical way. We have heat provided either by our landlord or by our own thermostat; water is as far away as the faucet; shelter is created by architects and builders; our clothes come off department store racks and our shoes from cardboard boxes. Like the little boy who thought milk came from the refrigerator, we have lost touch with the real origin of the things we use in everyday life.

Many of us have come to feel that this is not a good way to live and long to go back to simpler times; some of us, especially if we are younger, have taken to backpacking, living off the land, returning to the country. But on the whole we are not very well equipped for rural life, and of those who make the pilgrimage, a large proportion is forced back to more urban living.

This need not be the case; when it happens, it is due largely to bad planning, ignorance of what is involved, and trying to change too much too quickly. A knowledge of what you are undertaking and an understanding of the problems you will encounter will give you a much greater chance of success.

So it is with converting to wood as fuel for heating and cooking. I would like to see you pleasantly surprised, rather than unpleasantly disappointed after your first winter of heating with wood.

To this end, let me paint a less than glowing picture.

THE DISADVANTAGES OF HEATING WITH WOOD

1. *Wood is heavy.* Let us make no mistake about it. While handling wood—from cutting it up to stacking it in the woodshed—is well within the physical ability of an extremely elderly farm couple in good physical condition, it can be very tiring and demanding for a man who spends most of his time at a desk. The weight of wood is deceptive; a log is much heavier than you would guess from its appearance.

2. *Wood is bulky.* A winter's supply of wood should be laid in the spring and seasoned and stored at least until the following fall. Nine months is considered minimum storage for well-seasoned wood. This means a lot of storage space must be available for the woodpile. If such storage space is not available, you must be prepared to buy your wood in season and, therefore, pay top prices for it. Console yourself with the thought that even under these extreme conditions, it will still be your cheapest heating fuel.

3. *Wood fires need to be tended.* Even with automatic thermostats, wood fires need to be kept up by the addition of wood from time to time. The more time you can give to your fire, the more efficiently you can use your wood. There is also a certain amount of necessary adjusting to get the best energy (heat) return from your wood fire.

4. *Wood fires need to be laid and cleaned up.* When you get good at it, and if you have bought a really efficient stove, you need lay only one fire a winter—the first of the season. But you will still need to remove ashes occasionally and dispose of them; wood produces about sixty pounds of ashes for each cord of hardwood you burn. This isn't really very much and ashes are valuable in the garden for fertilizing and conditioning the soil. They are also good as a pesticide when dusted on plants, and if scattered around under plants, they will keep away slugs. (In talking about wood, it's hard to keep remembering that I'm trying to tell you about the disadvantages.)

5. *Chimneys need to be looked to.* When wood was commonly used as fuel, chimney fires were a frequent occurrence. Here again you can minimize the danger

and work by efficient burning. But even the best stove, well managed, will require that the chimney and venting pipes occasionally be cleaned; once a year is recommended.

A defective chimney is something that should be remedied before you build your first fire. A certain amount of soot and creosote buildup is unavoidable and cannot be neglected—a chimney fire is no joke.

6. *Wood stoves need to be maintained.* Some cast-iron stoves come with special finishes that do not require an annual stove-blacking. Otherwise you have to add that to your schedule. With sheet metal stoves, you need to check for thin spots, buckling, and other signs of wear.

At all times, you have to be alert for leaks, cracks, and other conditions that might require a bit of mortar or paint, or a new part.

7. *A wood fire produces heat that is variable and difficult to regulate.* Difficult but not impossible; in the beginning you are bound to have some failures. Wood heat is actually less variable than fuel oil—unless you have a thermostatically controlled wood-burning stove. Since the thermostat is activated by a drop in temperature, no heating system that works on a thermostat is going to deliver even heat.

8. *A wood fire is not easy to make automatic.* There are thermostatic controls in some stoves, but you sacrifice some of your heat and some of your comfort when you use them. If you are lazy with a wood fire, you pay a price. Chewing is work too, but we wouldn't give up a good steak for a diet of baby food.

If your schedule takes you away from home a lot, you may find a thermostatically controlled stove your best choice. There are fine ones available, and people who have them are very fond of them.

In other words, having a wood fire is a little bit like having children: only you can decide if the work is worth it. Most people who have given wood heat a chance decide that, like a family, it's well worth the extra work. Now for the other side of the coin.

THE ADVANTAGES OF HEATING WITH WOOD

1. *Wood is nonpolluting.* This is not a disinterested advantage. If we continue to pollute the atmosphere at the present rate, we will soon run out of air to breathe— certainly our children will. Many scientists and physicians suspect that a number of illnesses—in addition to the horrendous ones about which we already know—are being caused by pollution. They think we feel much less well than we should because we are breathing and ingesting so much that is inimical to the human body. The more people use wood for heat, the better off we all will be.

2. *Wood is inexpensive.* If it takes 141 gallons of oil to equal a cord of wood, and if oil costs forty cents per gallon, you can afford to pay over fifty-six dollars a cord for wood. If you burn wood really efficiently, you can pay up to seventy-two dollars a cord and still break even. Since fuel oil hasn't been as low as forty cents a gallon for over a year, and wood has cost sixty-five dollars a cord at its peak, you'd save money even if you bought all your wood. And buying all your wood is unnecessary—there is so much free wood to be had for the gathering.

These figures don't apply if you are burning wood in a fireplace; they apply to a well-designed, 80 percent–efficient wood-burning stove.

3. *Wood is available.* As we will see in a later chapter, there is plenty of wood in the United States, free, or practically free, for the taking. There is no reason why we shouldn't always have enough for our use.

If it becomes a question of priorities, it is even possible to look with equanimity upon a world devoid of paper napkins and paper cups. So far it doesn't seem as if it would ever come to that, but if it should, I think we would all survive it.

4. *Wood is a renewable resource.* It's up to us to grow enough for our needs; we've done it with citrus fruits, potatoes, wheat—we can do it with wood. And cutting wood actually will improve our forests and wildlife.

5. *Wood requires low energy for production.* Arm-leg-and-shoulder power is cheaper than the power needed to run the machinery to get fuel oil and coal from the earth to the marketplace.

6. *Wood requires no special facilities for storage.* Huge tanks, pipelines, extensive systems of distribution with concommitant high costs, all are done away with when you use wood. Many of us can go into our back yards for much of the wood we need; others can buy or gather it locally. In any case, all we need for storage is a little empty corner of land, a shed, or a cellar.

7. *Wood production is labor intensive.* There is comparatively little cash outlay involved in obtaining wood from the forest—whether you do it or your wood dealer does it for you.

8. *Wood warms many times.* This is a standard way of putting the fact that you work up a good sweat bucking, stacking, and lugging wood. I would rather say that it improves the health of anyone who has to deal with wood in any of its phases. Wood chopping is a great tension-reliever and does more than a dozen Valium to calm and relax a tense, frustrated, or angry individual.

9. *Wood is fulfilling.* All the benefits that are claimed for hunting, apply in spades to heating with wood—and you don't have to kill something in the process. There is tremendous satisfaction in pitting your strength and skill against the elements and warming your home and self with your own ability and effort. Yet the demands are not so great that there need be any strain in doing it. At least no more than in landing a large fish, or playing eighteen holes of golf on a tough course. There is a satisfaction in heating with wood that you cannot get in any of these pursuits, because what you are doing is not a game but an important and necessary contribution to the serious and challenging business of living.

10. *Wood is reliable.* Once you have wood heat, you will never again find yourself on the phone swearing at the electric company because everyone else in the neighborhood has heat and you don't. Or pleading with the fuel oil company to somehow get through to you even though the town plow has broken down and your road is under three feet of snow. Once again, being snowbound will be fun.

11. *Wood is beautiful.* You have only to see how reluctant man has been through the ages to give up the viewing of the open fire to realize how much it means to him. Whether it is due to some atavistic need, or just to aesthetic appreciation, fire has always been a symbol of home. Even the doughboys of World War I wanted to "keep the home fires burning." They surely were not thinking of the thermostat that turned on the fuel oil furnace.

Wood itself has an aesthetic value and handling it is pleasurable.

A WORD OF CAUTION

Although I have tried hard not to, I feel I have weighted the picture in favor of the wood-burning stove. So I would like to inject a note of caution.

If, after reading and considering the advantages and disadvantages, you

Antique French stove from the collection of De Dietrich & Cie. Photo courtesy of Pierre Weill, French Embassy.

have decided to go with wood, perhaps you should compromise and try wood as supplemental heating. In other words, do not quarrel with your fuel oil man, rip your thermostats off the wall, and install wood stoves in every room (not necessary in any case). Put in one good wood stove—the best you can afford to heat the area you have in mind—and plan to supplement it with your regular heating system whenever necessary. With that to back you up, you will be free to make a few mistakes, to decide whether heating with wood is really for you. You will be able to adapt your life-style gradually, tone up unused muscles. Don't burn your bridges along with your hickory logs—you may want to use them again.

Detail from antique French stove from the collection of De Dietrich & Cie. Photo courtesy of Pierre Weill, French Embassy.

4. Going with Wood— How to Do It

Wood burning—like gardening—is more of an art than a science. Even if you do everything according to the book, or the manufacturer's manual, you can still run into problems. Experience is the best teacher, and one of the first things experience teaches is that sometimes a correctly built fire in a good airtight stove vented into a properly constructed chimney will still not perform properly.

The unpredictable character of wood burning adds spice and variety to life; you will never again be content with the boring monotony of merely adjusting the thermostat. Wood burning is a small daily adventure, doubly enjoyable because it is ecologically sound and economically advantageous. And you will soon find that the glow of achievement you feel sitting in the cosy comfort of a room your own efforts have heated will be even more warming and satisfying than the actual heat generated—although at times that will be enough to send you around the room opening windows and turning down the draft.

The first step to achieving this happy state of mind is to understand the mechanics of what you are dealing with. The basic principles are simple, but somehow in application the variables involved make wood burning seem more complicated than it is. In any case, if you have ever tried to fix a leaky water closet, you know that simplicity is no indication of the difficulties you can encounter.

FOUR STAGES OF COMBUSTION

No matter what kind of wood you burn, it must pass through four stages of combustion.

1. *Removing Moisture.*

Even the driest wood contains approximately 20 percent moisture, which must be removed by heat; as long as it contains no more than 20 percent moisture, it is considered dry. Dry wood will not only burn faster than wet wood, it will produce more available heat, since heat required to drive off moisture is not heat that will do you any good.

Green or wet wood is very wasteful of heat. Where a cord of dry wood delivers 20 million Btu's, that same wood burned green will deliver only 16.5 million Btu's. In other words, green or wet wood actually has a *negative* heating value—it takes heat that you should be benefiting from, uses it to drive off moisture, and sends the evaporated moisture up the chimney flue. Old-timers may tell you that green wood is a good way to slow down or regulate a fire. Since it obviously is also a way to waste heat from wood you have had to cut, stack, lug, and store, there must be a better way.

Even with dry wood, the 20 percent moisture content requires the first few minutes of your fire to dry it out enough for it to burn efficiently. Green or wet wood can contain an incredible amount of moisture—more than 100 percent, which sounds impossible but has to do with the way moisture content is measured. The simple act of drying wood before you burn it produces so much more efficient fuel that it is foolish not to plan ahead so that you will always have it—at least after the first year.

2. *Breaking Down into Volatiles and Charcoal.*

Once the heat of the fire has eliminated moisture, the wood starts to break down chemically into volatiles and, eventually, charcoal. These are heat-producing elements in wood, and the more effectively you use them, the longer you keep them in your room, the more heat you will get from each cord of wood.

3. *Burning the Volatiles.*

Complete combustion of volatiles is not an automatic process. The importance of a good stove, a properly designed draft system, a good vent pipe, and a properly constructed chimney lies in the fact that their combined efforts result in burning these volatiles as completely as possible.

If your stove leaks, if your chimney stays too cold or does not draw properly even though it is not too cold, or if you do not understand how to regulate your draft system, too large a proportion of volatiles will escape up the chimney unburned. Not only will they fail to heat your house, they will also deposit soot and creosote on your chimney. The more volatiles burned within your stove, the more heat you will get from each piece of wood within the firebox.

Wood begins to break down chemically into volatiles at 300 to 400 degrees Fahrenheit. Complete volatilization does not take place until the wood in the firebox reaches about 1000 degrees; at this point it begins to form charcoal, which is the last stage of heat-producing combustion.

The best way to burn volatiles is to pass them down through the fire. Many downdraft stoves have been invented since Ben Franklin's vase stove, which tried to do just that. Unfortunately, heat wants to rise; so all efforts to force the volatiles back down through the fire are, so to speak, going against nature, and the results have been generally unsatisfactory. Most modern downdraft wood-burning stoves take the volatiles across, rather than down through, the flames. If you could invent a downdraft stove and circumvent the problem of back-puffing, you would not only be a better inventor than Franklin, you might even become more famous.

Obviously, if the volatiles rise from the fire and immediately go up the chimney, they are taking a lot of heat potential with them. The simplest devices for retaining the heat longer within the firebox are baffles; with them a greater proportion of volatiles are burned where they can do some good. In addition to baffles, some modern stoves have crossdrafts which they call downdrafts (perhaps on the principle that they hold the volatiles down and give the fire another chance to burn them and release more of their heat).

In studying diagrams of the flame path before you buy a stove, remember that the longer the flame path—in whatever direction—the more completely the volatiles will be consumed within the stove.

A fireplace is about 10 percent efficient. That means it utilizes about 10 percent of the heat potential of the wood burned in it; the rest goes up the chimney. A stove can be as much as 80 percent efficient—which means you are getting a lot more heat out of the same cord of wood if you burn it in a stove instead of a fireplace. The rate of efficiency depends, of course, on a good stove, a well-managed fire, and good wood. It also depends on how much oxygen is available to the fire.

As every schoolboy knows, it is impossible to have fire without oxygen. It follows that how and in what quantity oxygen is introduced into the firebox affects the efficiency of the fire. Too much oxygen means too hot a fire; too little means a smoldering fire. This is where the art rather than the science of wood stoves comes into operation. No matter how efficiently a stove is designed, you are the one who has to tend the fire and regulate the drafts, which let more or less oxygen into the firebox (unless you have a thermostatically controlled stove, which we will discuss in another chapter).

The amount of oxygen needed will vary, depending on the state of the fire. There are a number of variables, including the moisture content of wood, type of wood, whether it is split or in logs, whether it is a very cold day, a particularly windy day, and so on. Your judgment is on the line every time you adjust—or do not adjust—the draft. A well-managed fire is something to be proud of; it takes experience and skill.

4. *Burning the Charcoal.*

Charcoal produces only half of wood's heat potential. By itself it is not desirable as the main heat-producing factor.

Since you now know that much of the heat lies in burning the volatiles, you realize that for maximum heat you need flame—not just glowing coals. Charcoal does, however, play its part in a good fire. It helps to keep up the temperature in the firebox and chimney so that the wood burns more efficiently; it is useful for holding a fire overnight; and it eventually creates ash, which forms a good base for the next fire—in case you build more than one a season. (Many people who have learned to use their wood-burning stoves expertly do not.)

Incidentally, you may hear your neighbor brag about how long he has been able to hold his fire in the charcoal stage without adding wood—thirty-six hours is not impossible. Commiserate with him. He is creating a fire hazard unless he cleans out his chimney several times a season, and he is probably wearing extra sweaters.

A low fire is not desirable and should not be encouraged except where absolutely necessary—as for carrying heat overnight so as to have live coals for next morning's fire. The volatiles cool so much from a charcoal fire that by the time they reach the chimney they are moving slowly and deposit their soot and creosote there in large quantities. Not only will a charcoal fire give less heat, it will give more trouble. The manufacturers of Scandinavian airtight stoves, which have a good holding potential, always urge purchasers not to be carried away trying to break holding records, and not to use the stoves primarily as charcoal burners.

MAKING THE MOST OF WOOD'S HEAT POTENTIAL

A fireplace will deliver about 10 percent of the heat potential of the wood it burns. Devices designed to improve fireplace potential without sacrificing the beauty of the fireplace claim to increase this considerably. A simple box stove may provide 50 percent of the heat potential. An airtight stove or a real furnace, equipped with all the most sophisticated drafts and engineering, can deliver as much as 80 to 90 percent efficiency. These, however, are top figures; to make the most of whatever heating method you are using, certain factors have to be taken into consideration.

Types of Wood

As you can see on examining the tables on pages 175–176 (Heat Equivalents of Wood), the Btu's delivered by different species of wood vary considerably. A cord of shagbark hickory, a hardwood, will deliver as much heat as 251 gallons of fuel oil, whereas a cord of aspen, a softwood, will deliver the equivalent of only 128 gallons of fuel oil. In other words, it will take roughly twice as much aspen as hickory to deliver the same amount of heat. If aspen sells for one-half the price of hickory, it really costs about the same; also it requires much more work on your part—lugging logs to the fire, adding them, removing that many more ashes, and so on. Since a hardwood fire burns more slowly than a softwood one, you will have to add wood much oftener with aspen. Clearly, the best fuel wood is hardwood, and the consumer must make sure, if he is buying wood, that he specifies what kind of wood he wants and compares prices on that basis. If the dealer promises oak, don't settle for pine.

By the way, you will generally pay premium prices for white birch. This is because it is a luxury—decorative in the woodbox but a poor performer in the fireplace or stove. If you want a few pieces for show, keep them on display but don't burn them.

Dry Wood—How Important Is It?

Here we have to define our terms; dry wood generally contains approximately 20 percent moisture. This is the best you can achieve by air-drying the wood in an outdoor stack under normal conditions.

Wood is a naturally moisture-absorbent material. It easily reabsorbs moisture if given the chance. Conditions of storage are important and so is aging. Ideally, wood should not be used until a minimum of nine months after cutting, and twice that time is even better. Cut it in early spring or late winter and air-dry over the summer. However, as experienced campers know, if you must burn green wood in an emergency, yellow and black birch, sumac, white ash, and beech will burn better than other species.

On an average green wood is 70 percent less efficient than dry wood; it also builds up more creosote in the chimney. This means a considerable heat loss as well as more work and is well worth going to some trouble to avoid.

A covering of clear plastic in the summer will speed the drying process, providing you turn it over when it condenses on the side facing the woodpile. The plastic will make the air much hotter underneath than the outside air, and will retain the heat if the temperature cools down at night.

The high temperatures generated by the plastic covering will also discourage insects and help the wood to dry rather than rot. After a couple of months you will probably have to replace the plastic because constant exposure to the sun will deteriorate it; however, it is such an inexpensive material that replacement cost is a negligible factor. For a more permanent covering, once the wood has dried, construct a wooden lean-to or invest in tarps, which are practically indestructible.

By the way, if you live in a part of the country where wood is sold by the ton, insist on dry wood. A ton of air-dried hardwood such as oak, hickory, or maple is the equal of approximately half a cord. If it is green or wet, it will weigh much more and all you will be getting for the extra cost is moisture.

Wood Sizes—Room for Experimenting

In talking with a number of people who have been heating with wood for many, many years, I have been told with equal firmness that the best way to get the most heat out of wood is:

1. Cut it into lengths as short as can be conveniently used, splitting all sticks over three inches in diameter so that the average stick is less than three inches thick. *Or*
2. Use logs as large as you possibly can get into the stove—this obviously depends entirely on the size of the fireplace or stove door opening.

I go along with the second method. It saves a lot of splitting, for one thing;

and once you have a log burning well, it gives a slow, even heat for much longer. The smaller the piece of wood, the faster it will burn and the more often you will have to add more wood. Much as I enjoy tending a wood fire, I don't want to have to add wood any more often than is absolutely necessary. You might think that the manufacturers who have smaller openings might be the ones who advocate smaller wood, but this isn't necessarily so. Scandinavian stove manufacturers are all in favor of the second method, and they've had as much experience in burning wood as anyone in the world.

I suspect that a preference for one method over another is due to other factors—such as how the fire is managed. Since the management of a fire depends not only on what device you are using for burning the wood, but also on the nature of your chimney, the climate (cold and windy, or mild and breezy), and the nature of your installation, I would suggest you experiment and find which works best for your conditions.

I would imagine, also, that it would depend on how dry the wood is, what species it is, and what kind you can most easily and cheaply obtain.

Be Sure You Have a Good Draft

A house that is too tightly built can create problems by not bringing in enough air (and therefore oxygen) for good combustion. It is conceivable that this might happen in a house exceptionally well built and insulated for electric heat. In that case, you might have to open a window or put in louvers. This is rarely a problem, but even Ben Franklin was aware of it, so obviously the possibility exists.

Then there is a difference in stoves. Some have more efficient draft-control devices than others. A good draft means one that is just strong enough—not too weak, not too strong. If you have a roaring fire no matter what you do, you don't have a good draft—you have one that is too strong and you are wasting wood and heat. Before you throw out your stove for a new one, however, be sure it is the fault of the stove, not of the fire tender.

WHERE TO GET FIREWOOD FREE

Your Own Property

Obviously, if you own acreage in the country, you can supply some of your own wood needs. First cut up dead and fallen wood—this may keep you in fuel wood for years and will clear up unsightly litter at the same time. The next step is to identify and cut down trees which should be cut for good woodlot management. Your local State Forestry office will send a ranger to walk your land with you. He will advise you about which trees should be cut and on planting new seedlings and managing the land for maximum yield. Fast-growing trees, black locust for instance, can produce a sizable crop of long-burning, high-quality fuelwood in a remarkably short time.

In addition to advising you about harvesting fuelwood, the ranger may discover some valuable trees that should not be burned up. If you have black walnut, cherry, or oak trees, you may find a good market for cabinet-quality wood. Sawmills pay high prices for cabinet wood and will come and cut it down for you, as well as paying you for the wood. A nice windfall may be waiting in your back lot.

Property of Friends or Relatives

Even if you don't own enough of your own property to satisfy your fuelwood requirements, you may find that you can provide a service and obtain free firewood by clearing dead wood or cutting down unwanted trees from land owned by friends, relatives, and neighbors.

In this part of Connecticut it costs as much as two to three hundred dollars to have a good-sized tree cut down and carted away. If you are experienced and can cut down large trees, you can secure free firewood and be paid for it.

If you are not experienced enough to actually cut the trees down, you can still save your friends money by cutting up and removing the wood once the trees have been felled by professionals. Your friends will welcome your services and you will obtain free wood.

Dumps and Landfills

After ice and wind storms, the town and local residents dispose of fallen trees in local dumps. You are usually welcome to go and take whatever you want. The wood will usually have been cut into manageable sizes, and you will be surprised at how many truckloads can be collected free this way.

Private Landowners

In wooded areas you may easily obtain permission to remove dead and fallen wood. Sometimes a small fee will be asked, but most people are generous and will be pleased to have their woods cleaned up.

Your Own and Nearby State Forests

"Nearby" because you may live near a border. For instance, many Connecticut residents are near New York forest areas. Check with your Extension Service; they will know what wood is available and whether it is free for the taking.

National Forests

The U.S. Forest Service provides free permits for up to ten cords of dead, down, and unmerchantable fuelwood from national forest lands.

The Bureau of Land Management

The nearest district office will know about local conditions and whether there are any arrangements for gathering fuelwood in designated areas.

Telephone Company Cuttings

Keep an eye out for telephone company cutting. In order to minimize damage from fallen limbs, the telephone companies routinely clear out trees, leaving the cut material by the roadside for subsequent carting away. Anyone is welcome to it; you might as well be the one to benefit from this excellent source of good, free wood.

Hurricanes, Ice Storms, and Other Catastrophes

Much wood is downed, especially in the fall and winter, by weather conditions. The wood is usually hastily cleared and left on the verges for later collection. A tremendous amount of wood is available for the collecting.

You will be doing the town a service, saving your own tax money, and benefiting your woodpile if you systematically collect this debris.

Sawmills, Lumber Companies, and Wood-Related Industries

In this age of specialization, one man's garbage is another man's treasure trove. Since the cost of carting away waste materials is so high, and the room to dispose of them is so scarce, you can consider yourself a public-spirited citizen if you can recycle some of this waste in your wood-burning stove or fireplace. Don't collect a lot of trash or too much resinous wood; be selective. At the very least, you will acquire an endless supply of dry, already cut-up kindling; at best, you will lay in a good stock of fuelwood. Don't neglect chunk wood—it may look unfamiliar, but it makes perfectly good fuel.

Wood Dealers

The most expensive way to obtain firewood is, of course, to buy it already cut from someone who makes a business of selling it. Sometimes you have no choice because there is no other source, but even here you can effect a savings if you buy carefully. The following section discusses the various things you need to know to buy wood as reasonably as possible.

HOW TO BUY FIREWOOD

If all other sources fail and you have to fall back on buying wood from a local wood dealer, save yourself money by checking out the following procedures.

Shop Around

As with any other commodity, some dealers will charge more than others. It's worth making a few phone calls to dealers and asking your neighbors to find what the going rate is and who is offering the best deal.

Know What Wood You're Buying

Hardwood will cost more than softwood but will deliver more heat for the money. Ask what kind of wood the dealer is offering and check it out on the Btu's list on pages 175–176 to see how it rates.

You will need a smaller quantity of hardwood to get you through the winter. It will be easier on your chimney and stovepipe, will require less fire-tending, and will be more satisfactory in every way than softwoods.

However, if immediate cost outlay is the most important factor—and it may well be—try to get a mix of softwood and hardwood. It should be cheaper, but not all dealers will give you a cheaper price for less desirable wood unless they realize you know the difference.

Whenever possible, specify air-dried wood unless the difference in cost is prohibitive or you have time and facilities for long storage. Wood with a high moisture content burns less efficiently; much of its heat goes up the chimney. Fresh-cut wood—unless it is from dead or fallen trees—is green, and green wood makes a slow fire, not the sort of fire you want to wake up with on a bitter January morning.

However, not only green wood has a high moisture content; so does wood that has been improperly stored. Wood not kept under cover gets wetter with every rainy day or dewy night. Be sure you don't make the mistake, yourself, of buying good dry wood and storing it carelessly.

You will soon learn to recognize green wood from dry wood—in the beginning look for cracks radiating from the center outward; the more cracks the drier the wood.

Top left: *Standard cord of wood, measuring 4' × 4' × 8'*. Top right: *How to stack wood for quick-drying.* Bottom left: *12" run or face cord, measuring 4' × 12" × 8'*. Bottom right: *Unit or ¹⁄₂₄th of a cord. From* Wood as a Home Fuel, *Cooperative Extension Services of the Northeast States.*

Know What You Are Ordering

Wood is sold more often by a standard measure than by weight.

Cord. The most common measure is a cord, which is a stack of wood four feet wide, four feet high, and eight feet long—this adds up to 128 cubic feet, including air between the logs.

Run, Face Cord, Rick. For fireplaces or stoves, wood is usually cut into shorter lengths. These shorter lengths piled four feet high and eight feet long make up a "run," or "face cord," sometimes called a "rick." In other words a face cord of 12-inch-long wood would be twelve inches wide, four feet high, and eight feet long.

If a cord of wood is cut into 16-inch lengths, for instance, it will no longer measure 128 cubic feet because the shorter lengths will stack more compactly and will take up less room than the longer wood; also some of the wood will be lost in the cutting—how much can be judged by the amount of sawdust. On the average, if you are trying to judge a load, you can figure on a 10 to 15 percent loss in space, for instance, for four-foot wood cut into 16-inch lengths; 12-inch lengths will make a pile that is 25 percent smaller than the original cord.

Obviously, if you are planning to check on the size of the delivered load, you and the dealer should be clear as to whether you are talking about a standard cord or a face cord, and you should specify the length you want.

If you are able to cut up your own wood, you will save money ordering the standard cord in four-foot lengths; you will be able to check more easily if you have been delivered full measure, and you will have the use of the sawdust, which makes good compost and can even be burned under certain conditions.

Truckload. Some dealers sell wood by the "truckload." The amount of wood included in a truckload obviously depends on the size of the truck. Wood is surprisingly heavy—a cord of wood weighs between one and a half and two tons—and the typical pickup truck simply cannot hold a cord of wood. So beware of a "cord" delivered in a pickup truck.

If a truck has a six-foot body that is four feet wide and nineteen inches deep, it will hold less than one sixteen-inch run; if it has an eight-foot body, it will hold—at the most—one run. A full cord of four-foot wood would require a dump truck.

Incidentally, you always have to ask if the price of the wood includes stacking it for you, but with truckload wood, you will find that it is generally dumped and left to you to stack.

Unit or Carload. If you are picking up the wood in your station wagon or large car trunk, you won't be able to transport more than a "unit." This is usually two feet by two feet of sixteen-inch wood, about one twenty-fourth of a standard cord.

The cheapest way to buy wood is by the standard cord, but whatever you order you will find this is very much a case of let the buyer beware.

Measuring wood accurately is a bother, and many more-or-less honest dealers will estimate their load and perhaps not give you full measure. Any dealer who delivers a "cord" of wood in a pickup truck obviously knows better, and you should refuse delivery or arrange to pay for less than a cord. If the wood is stacked for you, check out the size of the pile before paying your bill; otherwise, stack it as soon as possible to see if you have received what you ordered. Also check whether it is all hardwood, if that is what you specified.

I wouldn't think it necessary to suggest that you avoid purchasing wood from roadside stands where it is sold to tourists at so much a log; but I have seen so many signs to that effect that I ought to mention that this is no way to buy wood if you are really serious about cutting fuel costs.

Buy Wood Out of Season

The biggest savings you can effect, if you have to buy wood, is to buy in late spring or early summer.

The wood dealer is probably busy then with other work—much of which is cutting and clearing trees. He will welcome the opportunity of selling wood he has on hand to make storage room for the new wood he is acquiring. By now you probably know what wood should cost in your area and are in a position to bargain if you are buying off-season.

The worst time to buy wood is from January on, when prices will be steadily rising. Try to anticipate your requirements and buy enough wood to carry you through until late spring. This kind of foresight requires you to provide storage space for a great deal of wood, but if you seriously mean to replace other heating fuels on a permanent basis, the sooner you set up wood storage facilities, the better. If you cannot provide a woodshed or lean-to of sufficient proportions, clear, heavy plastic cloths and tarps will do very well. (See next section.)

HOW TO STORE FIREWOOD

There are two kinds of firewood you will be storing—dry and green. With dry wood, the problem is to keep it from reabsorbing moisture; with green wood, the problem is to dry it.

Storing Dry Wood

Wood should be stored on a waterproof foundation; this can be concrete, brick, iron, or even wood that is not to be used. If possible, the foundation

Hall or Office Stove. Art Journal Catalogue of Crystal Palace Exhibition, London, 1851.

should be at least four inches above the level of the ground. This will create better air circulation and will prevent ground water from running under the pile and creating a wet atmosphere. Dry wood can be stacked fairly closely, but a thought should be given to circulation of air—your best drying medium in the open.

A roof or cover must be provided. This can be as elaborate as an enclosed shelter or as simple as a tarp or plastic. Plastic sheeting is available in large sheets; be sure to use a moderately heavy plastic—the drop sheets painters use are too thin—so that the edges of the logs won't cut through it and make holes that will admit rain.

If you are doing this for the first time, secure the covering by tying it down or anchoring it firmly after you have pressed it as closely as possible to the woodpile. That nice, mild, sunny day you picked to cover the wood is very different from the winter gale in which the tarp blows off in the middle of the night—the last thing you need to wake up to is a woodpile covered in two feet of snow. Even a well-secured covering should be checked every so often to make sure the wind hasn't worked a corner loose. Aside from moisture getting into the wood, moisture getting around the outside of the wood will freeze the whole cord solid, and you will have to use a crowbar to gather a stoveful.

If you are covering green wood, it should be covered in such a way that air can circulate in and around under the covering. On a really hot sunny day, you may notice moisture condensing under the plastic. If this occurs, remove the plastic for an hour or so and replace it with the damp side out; otherwise the moisture will drip down onto the wood and be reabsorbed.

Storing Green Wood

Follow directions for dry wood, with one big difference: in stacking green wood it is necessary to create greater air circulation. Ideally, green wood should be stacked alternately, with each log at right angles to the log above it, to form squares. After it has been stacked this way for about three months, you can stack it in the normal fashion.

If space is a problem, stack most of the wood in the usual way but put aside the wood you will need for the coming month and stack this alternately. It is really best to allow wood to season thoroughly before using, but this is not always possible.

Bring wood inside. Keep as much wood on an enclosed porch and as much beside—but not too near—the fire as possible. This will help to dry it out more than outdoor storage. Keep it away from the house wall, whether indoors or out. *There is one big exception to home storage:* if the wood is buggy or decayed, bring it in at the last minute. It would be better not to use wood in that condition at all, but sometimes there is no choice. In any case, always use your wood in order of its age—older wood first—so that insects have as little time as possible to take up residence. Badly decayed wood is no good as fuel; you won't be sold it, but you will have to examine wood you gather to make sure you aren't wasting time and energy dragging home a log that is good only for compost.

5. Wood Gathering and Harvesting– Tools and Tips

First look into wood stoves and decide which one to buy; then check the delivery date. Some stoves are in very short supply and, unless you have done your shopping early, may not be available for the first season you want one.

Once you have ordered your stove, ask your dealer to give you a rough estimate of how much wood you need to lay up for a season. Don't take his estimate too literally; actual needs may vary considerably, depending on how good you are at managing the stove, what kind of wood you can get, how much of the time the stove will be used for maximum heat, and many, many other factors. To be on the safe side, figure his estimate is a little short of the real thing.

Another way of estimating how much wood you will need is to check how much fuel oil you burned last winter. Then match this figure against your *Heat Equivalents of Wood* chart. Don't pick the greatest heat equivalents—take something in the moderate range. Since one cord of red maple is roughly equivalent to 190 gallons of fuel oil or 232,000 cubic feet of natural gas, you should be able to come up with a ballpark figure.

If you don't have the figures, ask a heating contractor to estimate how many gallons of oil your home would need for a comfortable winter; then figure a cord of hardwood as equal to 150 gallons of oil and you will have a safety margin.

No matter how you figure it, you ought to end up with something in the neighborhood of ten cords of wood. A farmer may use as much as fifteen to twenty cords—but that's figuring on wood heat only and includes a cookstove and some water heating.

Now you want to know how long it will take you to harvest ten cords of wood. That's like estimating how long it would take you to run a mile; it all depends on your condition, your training, your drive, and similar personal factors. If you're experienced and work at it full-time with a chain saw in top condition, you could do it in two weeks. Most people take longer.

In any case, don't rush right out and buy a chain saw. It is much more dangerous and demanding than a power mower, electric hedge trimmer, or roto-tiller.

USING A CHAIN SAW

As long as you understand that a chain saw is a potentially harmful device and know and respect its limitations, it can be a tremendous time-saver. In using it, however, be sure to observe the following precautions:

1. *Follow the manufacturer's instructions and cautions.* He knows his product better than you do—at first, anyhow—and he doesn't want a lawsuit on his hands. No matter how knowledgeable you are, take a minute to go over the printed material.

2. *Use the right fuel mixture.* Chain saws run on different fuels; your booklet will tell you the right one for the brand you have purchased. Don't substitute something else because you have it handy.

3. *Carry the saw by its handle.* Don't laugh—I've seen people tuck them under their arms when they had a lot of other stuff to carry.

4. *Do not transport the saw without a blade guard.* You'll tend to get careless about this, but it's well worth the extra minute it takes.

5. *When using the saw, hold it firmly and brace your body against the engine handle.* Occasionally the saw will pinch; it's better to be pushed than struck by the resultant action of the saw.

6. *If you're carrying the saw around, shut off the engine.*

7. *Don't use iron wedges.* Wood, plastic, or magnesium wedges will work just as well and they won't damage the chain as much.

8. *Wedge carefully.* Stop the saw and then wedge. If the wedge touches the moving chain, the chain may break, kick back, or stall the saw. If it kicks back, your face may be in the way.

9. *Watch out for knots.* A large number of chain saw accidents are due to the chain striking a knot. Try to saw in a clear area where the bark looks clean and smooth.

10. *Dress the part.* Sensible, well-fitting, not-too-warm clothing. Heavy shoes, boots with nonskid soles, shoes with toecaps, are all good footgear. Tennis sneakers are not.

11. *Get someone who knows how to handle a chain saw to check you out.* It's impossible to imagine some of the things that can go wrong when first using a new tool. Since chain saw injuries can be very serious, the best precaution is to have someone who knows how to check out your procedures the first time or two you use it.

OTHER EQUIPMENT NEEDED

Don't minimize the problem of getting the wood from its source to your woodpile. Commercial logging equipment includes tractors, pulleys, and other heavy machinery. Old-time farmers used horses and sledges. You may manage with your child's little red wagon—if you're only gathering wood from your backyard—but you'll make a lot of trips.

Wood is heavy and you're better off if you can make a rough "logging" road through your woods—something that you can get your pickup truck, station wagon, or lawn motor tractor through. Any way you can get transportation closer to the source of your wood, the better.

In the winter, if the site is right, you can make an old-fashioned sledge, rope pulled, and waxed or siliconed on the bottom to help it slide along easily even with a heavy load. They did it this way in the old days but with a horse; you won't be able to pull as much if you take the horse's place, but unless you have to go uphill, it's surprisingly easy to move a fairly heavy load.

On the site you have to decide whether you are going to buck the wood to size or just into more manageable pieces. That's up to you and depends on how you are hauling it; a station wagon works better with pieces cut to size.

Caution: *I can't emphasize too strongly that you have to be careful about overloading a station wagon, or even a truck. Wood is so heavy that you will have too much weight long before you have filled all the available space.*

In addition, if you decide to cut on the site, you will need:

a hand saw
an extra blade for the handsaw or a sharpener
a sharp axe
sledge or splitting maul
wedges

A Swedish handsaw of the bow variety works so easily and well that even an inexperienced woodsman can cut a lot of wood with it; it is very satisfying to use. The axe is for splitting and lopping.

If you take the wood home and cut it up there, add a couple of sawhorses to rest the wood on. In addition, I recommend some sort of log-splitter.

I'm not going to tell you how to use an axe; you can learn that best by getting some neighbor or handyman to show you. You'll get the knack of it in half an hour. Watching an experienced person swing an axe is like watching a good athlete; you have a model to emulate and you almost know how it should feel from how it looks. With someone right there to correct your swing, you will soon be splitting wood like an expert. And it's some of the best exercise going; you can still cut wood into your eighties, and you're much more likely to make it there if you spend some of your younger years in this healthful occupation.

Of course, any tool has to be handled with respect and an axe is no exception. A good woodsman will make this clear to you, so I won't belabor the point.

SPLITTING WOOD

Don't split wood unless you want it to dry quickly, or need smaller pieces for kindling, or the manufacturer says that the stove requires it—and even then, try both split wood and small logs to see for yourself which works better.

If you are seriously into wood burning, get a log-splitter. (See list of log-splitting equipment manufacturers in the appendix.) Some people make their own, but if you are good at that sort of thing, I won't have to suggest it. You can find articles in country magazines that will show you how to do it.

Log-splitters vary from simple manual devices to fairly elaborate and expensive ones that can handle commercial quantities of wood. Naturally the more expensive ones are faster and require less effort on your part, but unless you are planning to sell some of the wood you harvest, you don't need the more elaborate machines—certainly not in the beginning. If you have a neighbor who is also burning wood, you could share the cost and use of a log-splitter with him; you won't be using it so much that this would be inconvenient. (Of course, in this case, get one that is portable.)

TIPS ON WOOD GATHERING

Gathering wood is fun; the whole family can do it. Three-year-olds can pick up small twigs for kindling; wives, if they're willing, can do everything you can do except handle the very heavy pieces.

An important part of wood gathering is learning sources of free wood. (See pp. 52-54.) If you keep your eyes and ears open, you will find more opportunities than those I have listed; local conditions vary and an alert wood-gatherer makes the most of them.

Don't cut all your wood to one size unless you have only one use for it;

Nineteenth-century newspaper advertisement for stove merchant.

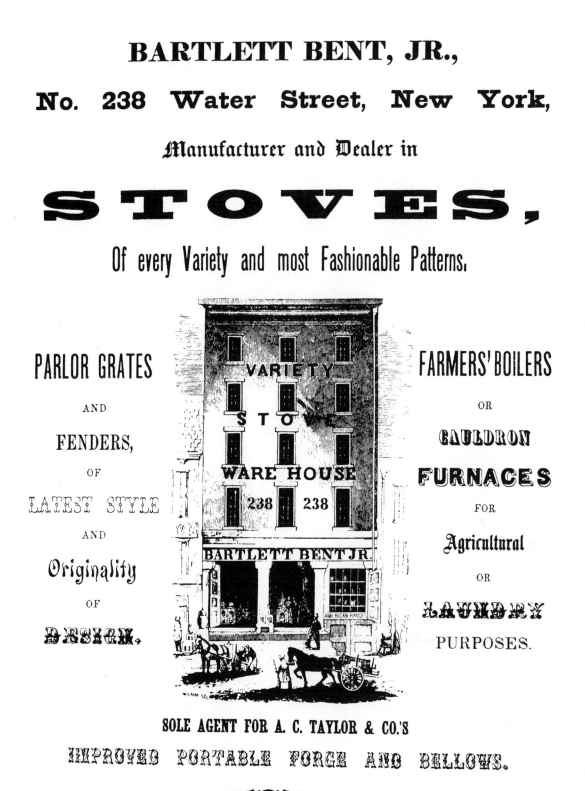

sizes should be smaller for cookstoves, larger for wood stoves, largest for fireplaces. Obviously, you need to know the size of your firebox in the first two instances—if you buck a stack of twenty-four–inch wood when your wood stove will take only sixteen-inch, you're in trouble.

Ideally, *wood should be split while green*. Dry wood is much harder to split. So determine how much you have to split and how much can be used as logs and then prepare it all accordingly.

Don't be stubborn about splitting wood. No matter how expert you are, some wood just isn't worth the struggle. Black locust, for instance, is practically impossible to split once it is dry—it's not easy even when green. Give up when you encounter a difficult piece of wood. You may injure yourself fighting that one log, and you'll certainly waste a lot of time.

Split wood if it is green and you are not going to have time to dry it properly—it will dry much faster than in log form.

Gather wood in clear weather. A cold clear day is better than a warm, rainy one. And cutting down trees on a snowy day is asking for trouble.

If you buy a chain saw, learn simple motor maintenance. There's no great mystery about how a chain-saw motor works, and if you have the intelligence to earn the money to buy one, you're smart enough to learn how it works. Simple motors get out of whack easily and chain-saw motors have a way of getting hard to start after a month or two. Usually all that is required is a small adjustment, and a neighbor can probably show you how to do it. If you have to take it in for repair, ask the mechanic to show you what was wrong and how he is fixing it. You could even get a handbook that would show you how to do a lot of the minor adjustments. Once you can keep it running yourself, you won't have it laid up in the shop just when you need it most. Of course, I'm not suggesting you turn into a full-fledged mechanic, but you should be as self-sufficient as possible. However, if you're still calling the plumber to put a washer in your leaky bathroom faucet, you probably won't want to take care of your own chain saw.

MANAGING YOUR OWN WOODLOT

If you have wood on your land and you haven't been practicing woodlot management, you can make it at least twice as productive by learning the right way to take care of it.

The government is eager to help landowners learn about better woodlot management and so is private industry. Call your Extension Service agent, ask him to tell you whom to call to get a ranger to walk your land with you, tell you what you should plant, how to deal with weeds and other undesirable growth, and mark the trees for the first cutting. He will also be able to tell you if you are eligible for seedling trees—they are available, at a nominal cost, to landowners who want to reforest their land. He will, at the same time, note valuable trees—these, of course, should not be burned.

In addition, there is the Tree Farm System. Write American Forest Institute, 1619 Massachusetts Avenue, Washington, D.C. 20036, for information about this industry-sponsored system.

6. Fireplaces: The Romantic in All of Us

As any backwoodsman knows, a campfire is better than no fire—but it is far from the last word as a heating device. No matter how the fire blazes, the best it can do is burn your extended fingers and your front while the snow settles, without melting, on your back.

When man invented shelter and moved his fire indoors, he first put it in the center of the shelter and trusted to a hole in the roof to get rid of the smoke. How well this succeeded in providing heat depended on how airtight the shelter was. In *The Friendly Arctic*, Stefannson, the Arctic explorer, described how efficient this type of fire was for the Eskimos:

To all intents and purposes the typical Eskimo . . . lives under tropical or subtropical conditions. The winter of 1906–1907 I recorded the estimate that the average temperature within doors of the Eskimo house in which I lived at the mouth of the Mackenzie River was . . . about 80 degrees F. and frequently rose to 90 degrees F. From the point of view of those who spent most of the winter indoors in that house, it was a matter of no consequence that the temperature was perhaps forty or fifty degrees below zero outdoors, when the outdoor air seldom came in contact with their bodies. . . . When an Eskimo comes into such a house . . . he strips off all clothing immediately upon entering, except his knee breeches, and sits naked from the waist up and from the knees down. Cooking is continually going on during the day and the house is so hot that great streams of perspiration run down from the face and body of every inhabitant and are being continually mopped up with handfuls of moss . . . and there is drinking of cup after cup of ice water.

It may be thought that Stefannson exaggerated somewhat in his effort to prove that one could be comfortable in the North, but he is not the only one to remark on the heat of the Eskimo igloo. Bartlett in *The Last Voyage of the Karluck* reports that the temperature within doors in the winter among the Northeastern Siberian Eskimos was an estimated 100 degrees Fahrenheit.

The Indians, on the other hand, were not so fortunate. Stefannson describes their living conditions:

In North America among the Indians, as one goes north from Mexico toward the Arctic Sea . . . their wigwams are cheerful with a roaring fire, but by no means comfortable. At night [they] go to sleep under their blankets, covering up their heads and shivering all night so that the blankets shake.

Both Indians and Eskimos had brought their fire indoors; one froze, the other perspired; wherein lay the difference? Since in both cases the fires were built in the center of the shelter and vented through a hole in the igloo or tepee roof, only two basic differences existed. Igloos, built out of solid blocks of snow with every crevice sealed firmly with ice, were completely airtight except for a tunnel-like entrance, which let in more than enough air to support a good fire. The wigwam, flimsily constructed of animal hides, had thin walls and no insulation, as well as numerous places where cold air could enter. In addition, the wigwam entrance was in the wall of the "room," and the cold air was drawn directly upon the inhabitants huddled around the fire, which increased the cold air currents the more merrily it blazed.

When our American colonists built their homes and fireplaces, they emulated the Indian rather than the Eskimo. Their fireplaces were large enough to stand in, and sometimes to sit in, but away from the fire outdoor temperatures prevailed. Cotton Mather, in his diary, tells of ink freezing in his pen as he sat and wrote *within the fireplace,* and another colonial diary describes how the sap forced out of burning logs turned to ice at the log ends.

Everyone is familiar with the charming stories of frontier childhood, where morning ablutions had to wait upon the ice being broken in the water pitcher, but not everyone realizes that this happened to basins of water standing on the hearth in front of a roaring fire.

Ben Franklin vividly describes the disadvantages of a fireplace:

1. People [must] crowd so close round the fire and [cannot] sit with comfort in any part of the room.

2. If you sit near the fire, you have . . . that cold draft of uncomfortable air nipping your back and heels . . . by which many catch cold, being scorched before, and, as it were, froze behind.

3. If you sit against a crevice, there is . . . that sharp draft of cold air playing upon you . . . by which many catch cold, whence proceed coughs, catarrhs, toothaches, fevers, pleurisies, and many other diseases.

4. The strongest heat from the fire, which is upwards, goes directly up the chimney, and is lost; and there is such a strong draft into the chimney, that not only the upright, but also the backs, sides, and downward heats are carried up the chimneys by that draft of air; and the warmth given before the fire, by the rays that strike out towards the room, is continually driven back, crowded into the chimney, and carried up by the same draft of air.

Not all colonists suffered from the cold; while the English colonists froze, the Dutch and German colonists were snug and comfortable. It may seem strange that English colonists would not have learned how to heat their houses when there were such successful examples all around them. However, the stubbornness of human nature is a very potent force against progress. The simple fact of the matter is that the English colonists liked to look at the fire; any device such as a stove that hid the fire from them was not acceptable— even if they froze dreamily to death in their enjoyment of the leaping flames. Ben Franklin, practical man though he was, typifies this approach in his description of the Holland stove:

Its conveniences are, that it makes a room all over warm. . . . Little fuel serves, the heat being almost all saved. . . . The air, too, is gradually changed, by the stove-door's being in the room, through which part of it is continually passing, and that makes these stoves wholesomer, or at least pleasanter than the German stoves. . . . But . . . there is no sight of the fire, which is in itself a pleasant thing.

And he feels the same way about the German stove:

The German stove is like a box, one side wanting. . . . This invention certainly warms a room very speedily and thoroughly with little fuel; no quantity of cold air comes in at any crevice, because there is no discharge of air which might supply, there being no passage into the stove from the room. . . . Its inconveniences are, that people have not even so much sight or use of the fire, as in the Holland stove.

Although Franklin preferred the open fire to the Dutch or Holland stoves, he did so in the face of his own common sense. As he says in another paper:

An English farmer in America, who makes great fires in large open chimneys, needs the constant employment of one man to cut and haul wood for supplying them; and the draft of cold air to them is so strong, that the heels of his family are frozen, while they are scorching their faces, and the room is never warm, so that little sedentary work can be done by them in winter. The difference in this article alone of economy shall, in a course of years, enable the German to buy out the Englishman, and take possession of his plantation.

Finally, when a wood shortage threatened Philadelphia, Franklin turned his inventive genius to creating a device that would provide more heat in proportion to the amount of wood it burned. He still, however, spurned the truly efficient Dutch and German stoves in favor of an open stove which would allow the fire to be viewed. It wasn't until forty-four years later, when possibly age and the accustomed comfort of European stoves had made warmth more important than viewing the flames, that he finally broke down and invented a stove that completely enclosed the fire—and even then, at the same time, he invented a special fireplace grate for use with pitcoal that would allow one to view the glowing coals.

This romantic attachment to an open fireplace persists even in this highly industrialized age. The English have long since given up burning wood for fuel, but they consider a house or apartment without an open fire as definitely lacking—even if the fire has to be artificial or electric.

Fireplaces in American homes are status symbols. And I once knew an art director in a New York advertising agency who insisted, as a mark of prestige, on having a working fireplace constructed in his suite of offices on the top floor of a large skyscraper before he would deign to accept his highly overpaid job.

Owners of New York brownstones are busily unbricking their fireplaces, and suburban homeowners point proudly to their new fireplaces, carefully constructed of expensive old brick and more or less unusable because they smoke so badly.

I have personally had many long discussions and arguments with friends and acquaintances who assure me that they heat their living or family rooms very comfortably with a fireplace. I give up.   There is no way that fireplaces can really heat our homes, and even if they could, they would waste so much heat and fuel that they are sheer luxury. However, since fireplaces are apparently here to stay, let us see how we can make the best of them.

DRAWBACKS OF A FIREPLACE

When fire first moved indoors, it was, as we have seen, placed in the center of the room so that the inhabitants could sit around it as they did with campfires. This proved inconvenient and clumsy, so it was next contained within its own niche—the fire was given its own place within the home and this became a fireplace.

Sometimes the fireplace was built in a wall in the center of the house with an enclosed chimney; sometimes it was built on an outside wall. More elaborate houses, with more than one room, had fireplaces that went through to an adjoining room—so that the keeping room and the living room might share a common fireplace with two hearths. Really large houses might have a fireplace in every room, including the upstairs bedrooms.

With these early fireplaces the chimneys were no more than straight funnels to the outside. Although early chimneys were sometimes made of wood, the constantly resulting chimney fires soon convinced the homeowner that this was not a practical way to build, and stone chimneys soon became common, except for the wealthier homes where brick was used.

In these early days the nature of combustion was not understood, and oxygen as such was unknown. Drafts and smoke were considered unavoidable inconveniences, and no scientific principles had been developed concerning them, so smoke shelves, dampers, and all the more efficient devices of later chimneys were not in use. As a result the fireplace invariably drew more cold outdoor air into the room than it contributed warm air. It still does.

In spite of his fondness for open fires, Franklin understood the drawbacks of a fireplace very well. He realized that a good fire requires fresh air to keep it burning strongly; since this air must come from outside, it creates drafts wherever it enters the room—through keyholes, window frames, crevices, and other unlikely openings. Anyone sitting between these openings and the fire is directly in the line of a cold draft and is chilled more than he is warmed. However, if all drafts are eliminated, the fire cannot get enough fresh air, and flags; the smoke, no longer heated sufficiently to rise up the chimney, comes into the room instead.

Unfortunately, due to the nature of a fireplace, most of the heat created rises in the form of smoke. If you send the smoke up the chimney, you lose most of the heat; if you don't send the smoke up the chimney, you will be warmer but asphyxiated.

Franklin estimated, fairly accurately, that at least five-sixths of the heat goes up the chimney. Modern engineers estimate that even the most efficient fireplace delivers only about 10 percent of the heat potential in the wood.

In homes heated by fuel oil or electricity, it has been shown that lighting a fireplace increases the amount of oil or electricity used. The fireplace draws air in to keep the fire burning; the warm air in the room is therefore lost up the chimney and cold air rushes into the room to replace it—from under doorsills, through improperly caulked window frames, around kitchen-fan outlets. As a result the air in the room is cooled and the thermostat triggered. Whenever you enjoy a fireplace in a house with central heating, you are upping your heating costs; the bigger the fire, the larger your heating bill.

However, if you do not have central heating and a fireplace is your only source of heat, you can make it as efficient as possible. First of all be sure the construction is as good as the present state of our knowledge can make it.

COUNT RUMFORD AND THE PRINCIPLES OF FIREPLACE DESIGN

Count Rumford, an American but a Royalist, came by his title through service to the Holy Roman Empire. He was inventive and original—very much like Franklin—and among his interests was the fireplace. He not only set down rules by which anyone could build a good fireplace; he went around rebuilding fireplaces that had been poorly built. Since most of the errors consisted in poor proportions and improperly designed chimneys, he was able to work with the existing structure and modify it rather than tearing it down and building it all over again from scratch. If you already have a fireplace that is not working well, perhaps you too can correct it. If you are building a new one, keep these rules in mind.

Count Rumford's Rules

1. *The chimney should have a smoke shelf.* In order to prevent backdrafts from cold air coming down the chimney, a smoke shelf should be constructed at the point where the chimney begins. This should be built from the back of the chimney toward the front.

2. *The damper opening—between the edge of the smoke shelf and the front of the chimney—should not exceed four inches.*

3. *The sides, back, and floor of the fireplace should be smooth.* Actually, Count Rumford recommended stone or brick for fireplace interiors; today the best material is firebrick. Firebrick is made of kaolin, a very fine quality clay that withstands extremely high temperatures—much higher than ordinary brick. It will give you a longer-lasting fireplace and will not crack or crumble from the heat of the hottest fire. It is such an ideal material for this purpose that many stoves are lined with it or have at least a floor of firebrick.

4. *The width of the front of the fireplace should be three times the width of the fireback.* A fireplace heats by sending rays directly into the room. Unlike a stove, these rays come into the room from only one direction and heat objects rather than the air. It is important to send out as many of them as possible—and as widely as possible. The best way to do this is to make the side walls of the fireplace, not at right angles to the back, but flaring outward. If properly built according to this three-to-one ratio, the walls will slant at the most efficient angle.

5. *The width of the vertical fireback (before it begins to slant toward the chimney) should be the same as the depth of the fireplace from front to back.* This will create a much narrower fireplace than you may be accustomed to; it will also place the fire in exactly the right spot to send most of the smoke up the chimney.

6. *The height of the vertical fireback should be approximately fifteen inches high before it begins to slant (or curve) toward the front;* it will end at the chimney, forming the floor of the smoke shelf.

7. *The front of the fireplace (from hearth to lintel) can be up to three times the depth (front to back).* This makes a very pretty fireplace because it gives an excellent view of the fire. However, it doesn't *have* to be that high—in modern houses with standard eight-foot ceilings, it rarely is.

My house, built fourteen years ago, contains a fireplace that conforms exactly to these specifications laid down in 1795; it draws beautifully and would delight all those who like to gaze into open fires. In addition it incorporates one principle important to efficient fireplaces but not listed above:

8. *The fireplace hearth should be flush with the floor of the room.* Since heat rises, the ceiling is the warmest part of the room, the floor the coldest. Sometimes fireplaces are built with raised hearths because they are decorative and allow the hearth to be continued on either side of the fireplace forming a convenient place to stack extra wood and to sit during a cocktail party. This is not efficient. A warm floor is so important that one of the best-selling devices for making fireplaces create more heat has an electrically operated blower that sends the air out beneath the grate into the room at floor level.

Now that you know how to build a good fireplace or to correct the one you already have, the next step is the chimney. Since a chimney is a whole subject in itself, I have devoted the entire next chapter to it.

You may want to skip to that chapter and then come back, because the next subject under discussion is how to lay and manage a wood fire in the fireplace.

HOW TO BUILD A WOOD FIRE

1. *Leave a shallow bed of ashes when you clean out the fireplace.* (Or save them in a bucket for next season.) They should be an inch or two thick; higher than that is bad for the andirons and could block the flow of air underneath the logs.

The ashes form a bed for the charcoal and keep it alive much longer. In fact, if you want to try to hold a fireplace fire overnight (hard to do), cover burning logs with ashes; you may have enough life in the charcoal to start a new fire in the morning by just raking the coals forward and adding kindling and wood.

2. *Open the damper.* This is so easy to forget that some people leave a permanent note tacked to the mantel, reading Open Damper. It's disastrous if you forget. The smoke will pour into the room because it has no place else to go, and you will have to reach over the smoking kindling to open the damper.

3. *Place crumpled paper, hemlock, birch bark, or cedar twigs on the ashes*, below the andirons.

4. *Add kindling.* This should be very dry wood; pine is fine.

5. *Arrange your logs horizontally or two horizontally and two in a sort of pyramid.* Use three or four logs; leave small spaces between them to promote a good draft. Don't use more than three or four logs. Add a little kindling at the center.

6. *Before you light the fire, light a spill of paper and hold it at the opening of the chimney.* The object is to heat the chimney, which will ensure a good, smoke-free draft. If you prefer, you can lay the paper on top of the logs and kindling and light it, but you should keep an eye on it. As soon as you see the smoke is going up the chimney, light the paper or bark on the ashes. If the chimney is cold, it will be harder to make it draw. In that case, put several small spills of paper on top and light them; then immediately light the paper or bark. You may get a little smoke, but it should be minimal.

A chimney in the middle of a house will heat up and draw more quickly than one on an outside wall.

7. *Do not build the fire too high or too close to the chimney.* Your fireplace has been constructed for a fire the depth of approximately two logs; if you build a high fire, you will be interfering with the operation of the fireplace.

It is not good if flames are so high that they reach into the chimney. There is bound to be some soot and creosote buildup after a while, and they could easily ignite and cause a chimney fire.

8. *Always replace the screen* when you are finished tending the fire. This is important even if you are burning hardwoods.

9. *Make sure the room is well ventilated.* Fire needs oxygen; a stuffy room will make a bad fire.

MANAGING YOUR FIRE

Your fire will provide the most even heat when some of the wood has turned to charcoal and some of the wood has small flames. The harder the wood, the longer the coal stage will last and the higher the heat within the fireplace will be.

To add wood, gently lay one or two logs on top of the burning fire. New logs should be added to the rear where they can reflect light and heat off the back into the room. If the middles of the logs have burned out, push the ends toward the center even if they fall below the andirons; or if you can manage it, lay them on top of new logs.

If Your Fire Falters

There are several reasons (other than a poorly built fireplace or poorly laid fire) why you may have trouble getting up a good blaze.

1. If it is very windy, even a perfectly built fireplace and chimney may not be able to cope with downdrafts.

2. You may have to adjust the position of your logs to create a stronger draft. Depending on the cause, try moving them closer together or farther apart (but not very much). You should see immediate results when you do the right thing.

3. Your wood may be too green or wet. There is nothing you can do about this except to try to use drier wood next time.

If the fire is going at all, it will dry out the wood eventually (although you won't get much heat while that is happening—and you may get a lot of smoke and sparks).

4. You may not have enough air entering the room. If you have a room that is tight as a drum, with no air coming in from outside, you won't have a very good fire because there isn't enough oxygen. Try opening a door or a window slightly.

TIPS ON COOKING WITH A FIREPLACE

Unlike our colonial ancestors, most people today who want a fireplace use it first to look at, second for heat, and—way down on the list—for cooking. However, if you want to try it, here are a few pointers.

If you have been camping, you know that the quality of food that can be prepared by burying potatoes and other vegetables directly in ashes is poor, if not downright inedible. We may have enjoyed charcoal-covered, half-raw baked potatoes in our very young scout days, but most adults wouldn't consider that food. However, if you have clay cookers, you can put the food in them, seal the cracks with clay, and pop them in the ashes—raked to one side of the fire. That works very well and produces superb meals—chicken, especially.

If you have an arm that swings over the fire, you can prepare soups, stews, mulled cider, and other goodies. A slow fire, without too much flame, works best; otherwise you will boil everything to death and it will be mush long before it is flavorfully cooked.

If you wish to barbecue or cook with a revolving spit, you will need special equipment because this should be done *in front of the fire rather than over it*. Any fireproof device that will allow a roast to be suspended in front of the fire, not too close but within range of good heat, with a dripping pan underneath, will do a fine job. (Be sure it is placed on the hearth or on an asbestos pad.) The only trouble is that this spit must be turned at least occasionally or the top part of the roast will drip all its good juices down to the bottom part and dry out to nothing.

In colonial days they sometimes had little dogs trained to walk in such a way that they turned the spit. There were also spits that were turned by a simple clockwork mechanism—and some, especially ingenious, that were turned by the smoke going up the chimney. The simplest method was to hang the roast by a string from the ceiling; whenever the cook had basted the roast with the liquid in the dripping pan, she gave the string a number of turns. As it untwisted, it naturally turned. This meant that it wasn't turning a good deal of the time and resulted in unevenly cooked roasts.

If you have an electric spit on an outdoor barbecue, you could rig it up with a drip pan to work in front of your fireplace. In any case, this is an area where your own ingenuity should get to work and solve the problem.

If you wish to broil, pop corn, or anything similar, you will need a very long handle to attach to your cooking utensil. You can rig up something with wire and a broom handle, or you may be lucky enough to find an authentic colonial handle in an out-of-the-way corner of an antique shop. A fireplace throws out concentrated heat in one direction so you will not be able to hold the typical iron frying pan over it the way you do with a campfire. The handle should be of wood, not metal, but should be attached to a metal handle that sits over the fire.

If you allow grease to spill into the ashes on the hearth, you will have a fine mess to clean up and you will *have* to clean it up or the smell will permeate the whole house in a very few days. Some modern Franklin fireplaces have accessories that allow you to grill in them, but the manufacturers don't seem to supply drip pans. I asked one of them what happened to the grease and never received an answer. Offhand, I should think grease buildup on the floor of a stove would be a fire hazard, and I would suggest that you put down an old broiler bottom or cookie sheet to catch the drippings.

FIREPLACE SAFETY

An open fire is more of a hazard than an enclosed one; the Consumer Product Safety Commission lists fireplaces as the 127th most important hazard in its list of 369 hazards. Since this list includes bicycles (No. 1 hazard), automobiles, power tools, and other widely used items, even this rating isn't a fair indication of how dangerous fireplaces can be. If as many people used fireplaces as drive cars, they would be much higher on the list. Here are some factors to keep in mind:

1. *Be sure your chimney is reasonably clean.* If you use a fireplace only occasionally, it will stay clean almost indefinitely. Regular, frequent use means an annual checking—and probably, cleaning—due to buildup of soot and creosote. (See Chapter 7 for cleaning suggestions.)

2. *Be sure your chimney is in good condition.* A clogged or leaky chimney not only makes it impossible to have a good fire but is also a fire hazard.

3. *Don't use fire starters.* We're so used to using fire starters for barbecues that it is often automatic to reach for one when starting any fire. Don't. A properly built fire in a properly constructed fireplace with a well-built chimney doesn't require anything more than a couple of matches; in fact, the fire will start faster with the matches alone.

4. *Be sure the damper is open before you light the fire.* I've already talked about

this, but it can't be said too often. Do it before you even start to lay the fire; you're less likely to forget.

5. *Don't burn trash.* A fireplace isn't an incinerator. Here in Connecticut, when a law was passed forbidding outside burning of trash in incinerators, it simply moved indoors. Homeowners routinely throw the contents of their wastebaskets into the fireplace. This is not good practice; it will build up creosote and soot in your chimney and often overheat it. Bundle up your trash and cart it to the town dump; the fireplace is for wood.

6. *Use a fireplace screen.* Fire and sparks belong in the fireplace, and the only way to be sure of keeping them there is to place a screen in front of the fire that is large enough to cover all of the width of the fireplace opening. Even if you use dry hardwood, impurities may cause popping. In addition, a sudden gust of wind outside may cause a backdraft down the chimney and scatter sparks.

Never leave an open fire alone without a screen in front of it—even if it has practically died down.

7. *Hardwoods are safer than softwoods.* Aside from all the other reasons why hardwoods are more desirable as fuel, they are safer. Softwood has pockets of moisture within the wood; when heated, they create gases and water vapor, which become trapped inside. The pressure builds up and releases itself with popping, scattering sparks in all directions.

Softwoods make good kindling, however, and that is perfectly safe because you don't use much of it and it is burned up very quickly.

8. *Don't leave children alone in a room with a fire.* Especially someone else's children—yours may be trained to fires. Children are a little unpredictable and warning them not to do something may be a sure way to make it happen.

7. What Goes Up a Chimney? Smoke!

Whether you heat with wood, coal, gas, or oil, in a fireplace, stove, or furnace, you must vent your heating device to the outdoors. The usual method is through a chimney or, if you don't have a chimney, through a stovepipe. This chapter will deal with the functioning—and nonfunctioning—of a chimney.

Since the function of a chimney is to draw off the volatiles created by the fire, it must first of all draw well. However, if it draws too well—i.e., too strongly—it will burn up your wood in record time with little benefit to you in the way of heat. It may also let in a great deal of cold air. It may draw poorly and cause the fire to die down, or even go out; it may let smoke seep back into the room, or even, with downdrafts, drive it back into the fireplace or stove.

In addition, a chimney should warm up quickly and not cool off too fast; it should minimize smoke, wind, and temperature changes. Since a chimney is not a living thing, these situations are presumably all under your control; unfortunately, in actual practice, not all of them are.

CHIMNEYS AND TOPOGRAPHY

You cannot always choose where you will build your house just to suit the chimney.

If you like a house nestled at the foot of a hill, or just on the edge of an extended forest, you are creating some problems for even the best chimney. The trouble is that chimneys are affected by air currents, and air functions, to some extent, like water. If a chimney is at the foot of a hill, the air runs down the hill and pours into the chimney; if it sits at the edge of an extended forest, the wind runs along the top of the trees and drops abruptly into the chimney as it comes to the cleared area.

Similarly, if you have a house in a built-up area with many tall buildings around you, some of these same problems will exist. In any of these instances, the best you can do is put on a chimney cap to deflect the air; you might even consider a revolving cap, which will turn some of the wind power to your advantage.

However, an occasional back-puff, a bit of smoke when a fire is first started, is only to be expected. What you are aiming at is a fire that in the long run draws steadily, maintains constant heat, and burns as near to 100 percent combustion as your heating device is capable of—a good chimney should accomplish all these things.

MASONRY CHIMNEYS

If you have a fireplace or a furnace for central heating, you probably have a masonry chimney. This can be used to vent a wood stove by following the manufacturer's directions, which come with the stove. If you do not have a chimney and want to build one, there are government and Extension Service booklets that will tell you exactly how. Always check with local town ordinances; they sometimes have special requirements.

Location

If you are building a chimney from scratch, consider locating it in the middle of the house instead of on an outside wall. A chimney on an outside wall is a

STAR SUNSHINE COOK.
For wood only, with Reservoir.

The Star Sunshine is a beautiful cook stove with all modern improvements. It is heavy and durable. In practical working qualities it is unsurpassed.

The special features are: Handsome skirting, portable outside oven shelf and extended rear shelf, nickeled oven door opener, large nickeled oven door plates, extra heavy covers and centers, tinned lined oven door, top oven plate inlaid with non-conducting plaster composition, nickel tea pot stand and towel rod.

The Star Sunshine is one of the best wood cook stoves in the country. The reservoir has a large capacity and heats water quickly. The Star Sunshine is a first-class stove in every particular. Length of fire box given below is the size when stove is ordered to be used for wood. Has four covers. No. 15832.

No. 15832.

$3.50 for a set of No. 8 Stove Furniture, to fit any of our cook stoves.

$3.75 for a set of No. 9 Stove Furniture, to fit any of our cook stoves. See Tinware Department.

Size.	L'gth Fire Box. Covers.	Size of Oven.	W'ght.	Price.
8	8 in. 20 in.	18x18x11½	240 lbs.	$12.60
88	8 in. 22 in.	20x20x12½	270 lbs.	14.70
9	9 in. 22 in.	20x20x12½	273 lbs.	14.88
888	8 in. 24 in.	22x22x13½	310 lbs.	16.30
19	9 in. 24 in.	22x22x13½	313 lbs.	16.68

No. 15833. The Star Sunshine Cook, without reservoir—otherwise like cut.

Size.	Oven.	Weight.	Price.
8	18x18x11½	195 lbs.	$ 9.54
88	20x20x12½	225 lbs.	11.28
9	20x20x12½	228 lbs.	11.40
888	22x22x13½	255 lbs.	13.62
19	22x22x13½	260 lbs.	13.80

Prices named for Stove do not include Pipe or Stove Utensils. Make your own selection from our catalogue.

"One of the best wood cook stoves in the country." Sears, Roebuck and Co. Catalogue, 1897.

handsome addition to the appearance of your house; it is also unnecessarily costly and not nearly so efficient. The large area exposed to the cold outdoor air makes the chimney harder to heat up and harder to keep warm. Because the air will cool faster, the volatiles will deposit more soot and creosote on the sides of the chimney, and it will need to be cleaned much more often. Also, the mortar will weather faster and need to be pointed much more often. All in all, I would strongly urge you to sacrifice the purely decorative in favor of utility. I can think of no practical advantage to an outside chimney.

Height

Starting from the top down, one of the most important aspects of your chimney is its height in relation to surrounding objects. It should be two feet higher than any roof ridge within ten feet, three feet higher than a flat roof.

If your chimney is not high enough, this can be easily remedied without any major rebuilding. Do not, however, make the mistake of thinking the higher the better; a chimney that is too high may be knocked over by strong winds; it may also allow the volatiles to cool too much in the exposed area, thus creating an unnecessarily fast buildup of creosote and soot.

Flue

The flue is the part of the chimney in which the smoke rises; it extends from the top of the smoke chamber to the top of the chimney. Ideally, each stove or fireplace should have its own flue; a stove should never be vented to a flue which also vents an oil-burning furnace. While it is sometimes allowable to vent two or more heating devices on one flue, it is never desirable, and you must be sure your local fire laws permit it.

An old chimney that is built of stone or brick may not be lined; if at all possible your chimney should have a flue liner—otherwise mortar and bricks will be acted upon by flue gases and eventually deteriorate, necessitating major repairs. All old chimneys should be tested for leaks; not only will they affect the draft, they may cause fires.

Flue linings are made of fire clay and should be at least five-eighths of an inch thick. They may be installed after the chimney is built, but it is difficult to do so.

Smoke Shelf

Count Rumford knew all about smoke shelves and corrected many a fireplace merely by adding one. The function of the smoke shelf is to keep cold air and smoke from coming *down* into the room—in other words, to prevent downdrafts. Because of its construction, it also creates movement of air within the chimney, mingling the cold air of the downdraft with warm air from the fire and thus maintaining the heat of the chimney. Count Rumford's rule is still considered good practice today—the smoke shelf should be built from back

Dutch Hall Stove. Art Journal Catalogue of Crystal Palace Exhibition, London, 1851.

to front, and the distance from the end of it to the front of the chimney should not exceed four inches.

Damper

From the beginning of its conception a chimney was a great improvement on a hole in the roof, but its usefulness and efficiency was increased immeasurably by the simple invention of the damper.

Both Dr. Franklin and Count Rumford—without reference to each other —dealt at length with this invention. Dr. Franklin described it as follows:

An iron frame is placed just under the breast and extending quite to the back of the chimney, so that a plate of the same metal may slide horizontally backwards and forwards in the grooves on each side of the frame. This plate is just so large as to fill the whole space, and shut the chimney entirely when thrust quite in, which is convenient when there is no fire.

Count Rumford had much the same idea, but he developed it more fully and in the form that is used today in well-constructed chimneys.

Chimneys should always be built with dampers. They are usually of cast iron with a hinged lid that opens or closes across the area where the smoke shelf ends.

The functions of a damper are fourfold:

1. *To regulate the draft* by varying the size of the opening.

2. *To prevent loss of heat from the room.* When there is no fire or it is very low, warm air will be drawn from the room and be lost up the chimney; cold air will come in one way or another to replace it; if you are using the fireplace for supplemental heat, the furnace will turn on to create more warm air, which will go up the chimney. You can use up a lot of fuel oil this way and still suffer from a chilly, drafty room.

3. *To regulate the fire.* A blazing fire may be best obtained by opening up the damper completely; a slow-burning fire will be maintained best by a much smaller opening. By regulating the opening to the smallest size that will provide the type of fire you want, you will minimize heat loss.

4. *To shut the chimney.* In the summer when the fireplace is not in use, the chimney should be shut completely. This will protect the room from an invasion of insects such as elm bark beetles, which sometimes almost literally pour down a chimney; from birds that have unaccountably lost their balance and fly with soot-blackened wings all around your freshly painted living room; from rain, wind, and other uninvited guests.

I'll never forget the time my two boys, who had been put to bed with some difficulty on a beautiful summer evening, called down that there was a big black bird walking on the floor of their room. Don and I thought it was just another ploy to stall having to settle down, and it took a couple of insistent calls before we went up to investigate. We found each of the boys barricaded on their respective beds behind hastily erected blanket shields, while wandering around the room in considerable bewilderment was a huge black crow. We'll still never figure out how he got down the bedroom chimney (we could have sworn the damper was shut), but there he was; and I have never seen a crow look so big as that one did that night. It wasn't easy getting him out.

I have often thought that it would be handy to have some way of closing the summer chimney closer to the top so that chimney swifts and such could easily be evicted by reaching one's hand down a few inches instead of having to get down several feet. At present, however, no one has invented such a device, so we must make do with the damper.

There are a number of different dampers on the market and your builder and architect should be consulted as to which they think is best—but find out their reasons before you agree to their choice; some dampers are better than others and worth the difference in cost.

Weight

Chimneys are very heavy and require good support. Almost no frame house built today has a floor that could support a chimney. Of course an outside chimney does not rest on floor joists and therefore should be built on solid ground below the frostline. An inside chimney is usually built right down to the basement where the ash box is incorporated with a door for ash removal. However, if there is no basement, the chimney must extend into earth and go below the frost line.

Aside from anything else, the weight of a masonry chimney requires that the builder have a good understanding of the stresses and fire hazards involved. (An inadequately supported chimney will settle, creating cracks that constitute a serious fire hazard.)

Insulation

A stone or brick chimney that is unlined may provide heat throughout the house as it goes up to the roof, but the potential fire hazard it creates is not worth the extra heat. It is extremely important that no wood come in contact with the chimney—even a lined chimney. This rule applies to flooring and subflooring as well as to walls. Do not underestimate how hot a chimney may get, and take into account the unhappy possibility of a chimney fire.

Roof

Special care needs to be taken where the chimney comes through the roof. Water must be deflected away from the chimney if the pitch of the roof drains water onto it. This device is called a cricket and is installed along with the flashing, which makes the area immediately around the chimney fireproof and creates a tight seal so that water will not leak into the house.

Construction

I do not intend that the above discussion will make it possible for you to actually construct a chimney. There are how-to books and government booklets that will give you the specific measurements and information you need; I only want to give you a little general knowledge about chimneys so that you can look at them with a somewhat more knowing eye.

Cleaning

All chimneys need to be cleaned of the deposits of creosote and soot that any fire deposits on them. How often cleaning is required depends on a number of factors:

How often you use the chimney;
How well you tend your fire;
How good your stove (or fireplace) is;
What kind of wood you burn;
Whether your wood is dry or wet;
How often the fire is banked or allowed to die down;
How windy it is;
How cold it is.

Only experience can tell you how often your chimney needs cleaning, but you should figure on once a year at the least, unless you are using it only for an occasional fire in the fireplace.

Cleaning a chimney is something you can do yourself if you are handy at that sort of thing. You may not want to bother—in which case, ask around for a chimney sweep.

In the old days chimney sweeps were little boys or small, undersized men who were sent up a chimney with brooms and cloths to actually "sweep" it out. They were often suffocated by the material they were sent up to remove; they frequently got stuck in the chimney and were dragged down more dead than alive. They were subject to "consumption," infections, and divers unpleasant illnesses and were usually short-lived. Modern chimney sweeps never actually go up the chimney.

If you wish to try to clean your own chimney, the first step is to close off the fireplace opening so the creosote and soot you dislodge will not come out into the room.

The next step is to get up onto the roof in a secure position so that you will not fall off. On a steep-roofed colonial saltbox, this is harder than you might think.

There are a number of ways to clean a chimney, and you might have to try a couple before you find the one that suits you. They are all based on the same principle: lowering something into the chimney and then drawing it up and down so that it hits against the sides and knocks the creosote and soot loose.

In colonial days a live goose was sometimes used. As it was lowered and raised, it beat its wings, thus loosening the caked-on material. Another device was to lower a chain tied to the end of a rope—this is still popular today. With this method there is a certain amount of risk—especially if you are dealing with a brick or stone chimney—that you will loosen mortar as well as soot, but perhaps you can develop a firm, gentle touch; and you will not be able to swing the chain excessively because of the confines of the chimney itself. Another recommended device is to lower a fresh-cut evergreen tree headfirst; as you draw it back up the chimney, the branches will spread out and act like a brush. This is surprisingly effective if you haven't baked on the creosote too firmly.

Whatever you do, attach your cleaning device securely to your rope; a friend of mine tried a bag of rocks attached to a rope. It was a small bag of fairly small rocks, but somehow it broke off the rope and wedged firmly halfway down the chimney. He had the devil's own time getting it out.

You will know your chimney is clean when no more stuff drops down into the fireplace. It helps to have someone check it out for you so you don't have to keep clambering up and down the roof.

Chemical Cleaners

There are chemical cleaners on the market to sprinkle on a fire; they are supposed to clean the chimney, but the results are not always satisfactory. One problem is that the creosote will melt when it comes in contact with the heat and will not only make a mess of your pipes and stove, but may also damage your stove material. The Department of Agriculture, in its bulletin on fireplaces and chimneys, says:

"Chemical soot removers are not particularly recommended. They are not very effective in removing soot from chimneys and they cause soot to burn, which creates a fire hazard. Some, if applied to soot at high temperatures and in sufficient quantity, may produce uncontrollable combustion and even an explosion. Common rock salt is not the most effective remover, but it is widely used, because it is cheap, readily available, and easy to handle. Use two or three teacupfuls per application."

In addition, no tests have been made of the long-range effect of chemical chimney cleaners on the interiors of chimneys—unless you have no other recourse, I suggest you try some other method.

PREFAB CHIMNEYS

If you are installing a wood stove or a free-standing fireplace, you may do so without a chimney to vent into. In this case, there are chimneys you can buy that are completely prefabricated and come with very complete installation instructions, which you should follow to the letter, after first checking with your fire department.

SMOKY CHIMNEYS

Like the television repairman who always told housewives in distress to be sure the set was plugged in, any discussion of smoky chimneys should start with the advice, "Take a look." This doesn't mean you necessarily have to climb into the fireplace—a strategically held mirror will give you a good view. Do it on a clear, sunny day; if you don't see daylight, investigate. Birds love to build nests in chimneys; bricks or mortar can work loose and prevent the flue from drawing properly; various things can get lodged inside; so it only makes sense to check out the easiest possibilities before going on to more complicated ones. Also, there is always the chance you could have sworn you opened the damper—but you didn't.

If, however, all the above are in order, we have to consider other possibilities.

Ben Franklin, in 1785, wrote on the "Causes and Cures of Smoky Chimneys," and most of what he had to say is equally valid today.

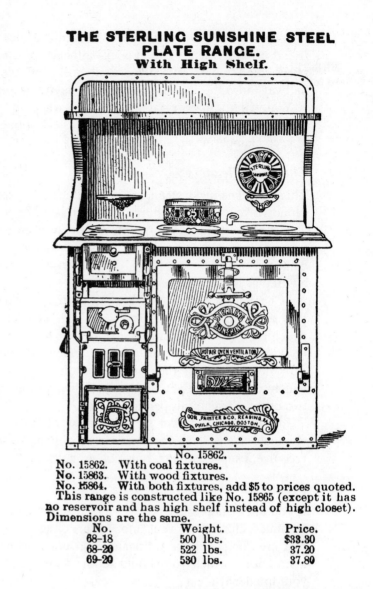

THE STERLING SUNSHINE STEEL PLATE RANGE.
With High Shelf.

No. 15862.

No. 15862. With coal fixtures.
No. 15863. With wood fixtures.
No. 15864. With both fixtures, add $5 to prices quoted.
This range is constructed like No. 15865 (except it has no reservoir and has high shelf instead of high closet). Dimensions are the same.

No.	Weight.	Price.
68–18	500 lbs.	$33.30
68–20	522 lbs.	37.20
69–20	530 lbs.	37.80

". . . No devices for mere show and appearances, but it has every good feature that will promote utility, convenience and durability."
Sears, Roebuck and Co. Catalogue, 1897.

1. "Smoky chimneys in a new house are such, frequently, from mere *want of air* . . ." This is especially true of fireplaces that draw large quantities of air, but it also affects proper working of wood stoves. To determine if this is the problem, merely open a door or window a little and see what happens. If the smoke then goes up the chimney instead of into the room, adjust the opening until it is as small as it can be and still work. If necessary, louvers can be installed in a window so that air can be provided without draft. However, this is rarely the cause of smoky chimneys in today's houses.

2. *"Incorrect proportions of fireplace or chimney . . ."* Franklin, in his usual meticulous way, broke this down into "openings in the room being too large; that is, too wide, too high, or both . . . ; too short a funnel . . . and too low a chimney."

If you are dealing, not with a fireplace, but with a stove vented into a fireplace or directly to the outside, you may encounter additional problems; the size of the

THE STERLING SUNSHINE STEEL PLATE RANGE.

With high closet and reservoir for hard or soft coal or wood. To meet the demand for a steel range we offer the **Sterling Sunshine**, in which is combined solidity, durability, efficiency and convenience. It has no devices for mere show and appearance, but it has **every good feature** that will promote **utility, convenience** and **durability. Special features:** The entire outer body is one piece of heavy, cold-rolled wrought steel. Inside the outer body there is a wall of asbestos (the best non-conductor known), and inside the asbestos a lining of sheet steel. All other parts of the range (except the oven) are also lined with asbestos. This method of construction concentrates the heat in the oven and secures an economy in fuel never heretofore attained. The top rim is cut in four sections. The slip plates, covers, and cross pieces are heavy and durable. The reservoir holds 15 gallons and the water is heated by a half-size water front by circulation, which does not interfere at any time with baking. Has six holes.

No. 15865. With coal fixtures.

No. 15866. With wood fixtures.

No. 15867. With both fixtures, **add $5 to** prices quoted.

We can furnish this range without reservoir. If ordered without reservoir, deduct $8 from prices quoted.

No. 15865.

No.	Size of Covers.	Size of Oven.	Size of Top.	Weight.	Price.
68-18	8 in.	18x14x22	36x30	550 lbs.	$44.40
68-20	8 in.	20x14x22	39x30	585 lbs.	48.30
69-20	9 in.	20x14x22	39x30	590 lbs.	48.90

Send for our Special Catalogue on Steel Ranges.

flue, the nature of the pipe connecting the stove to the flue, the direction of the stovepipe, and so on.

3. *"Improper and inconvenient situation of a door."* Here again this is more likely to be a problem with a fireplace than with a wood stove. Since air entering the fireplace opening is a factor, too much is as bad as too little. A door directly opposite a fireplace may create too strong a draft. If you are building a fireplace, try to situate it so that this does not arise.

4. *Back-puffing.* "A room that has no fire in its chimney is sometimes filled with smoke which is received at the top of its funnel, and descends into the room . . . driven down by strong winds passing over the top of the funnel." We've already discussed this in some detail under *Chimneys and Topography*. Closing the damper will eliminate the problem.

If it occurs when you have a fire going, try some sort of chimney cap.

5. *Competition with another fireplace.* In colonial days it was not uncommon to have two fireplaces in one room or in adjoining rooms. As a result, one might, in Franklin's words, "outdraw the other." The loser in the game would send its smoke out into the room instead of up its chimney. I don't think this would be a problem today, except perhaps in a hotel lounge or clubhouse.

6. One factor you always have to deal with is a *cold chimney. A cold chimney will not draw*, so a certain amount of smoke is to be expected whenever you start a new fire or activate a banked one. This is the reason you should start a new fire by first burning a twist of paper on top of your new-laid paper and kindling, or activate a banked fire by opening the damper to its fullest extent and allowing a greater draft than normal.

7. *Leaky chimney.* Anything which interferes with the orderly passage of air up and down the chimney may cause the chimney to smoke. Leaks in the flue create unplanned drafts and are not only a serious obstacle to a good draw, but a fire hazard. They can sometimes be detected by temporarily stopping up the chimney's top opening and watching to see if smoke escapes where there should be no opening. However, this test is not practical for chimneys on inside walls—unless you have cracks in the walls, floorboards, or baseboards. If not, only an inch-by-inch inspection of the flue will do. I have put this cause last because it is the most expensive and troublesome to fix; I would suggest you exhaust all other possibilities before settling on this one.

The only sure way of discovering the cause of a smoky chimney is trial and error. You may be lucky and correct it on first try; you may struggle with it for a red-eyed, teary week before you call in expert help—who may or may not do any better than you did. Experience with wood fires will give you a feel for what is wrong. Keep in mind, however, that chimneys smoke for many different reasons, and these can change. If you have checked out construction, you still have to deal with wind and temperature variables.

Even Franklin goofed once in a while, as in this story he cheerfully told himself.

Another puzzling case I met with at a friend's country house near London. His best room had a chimney, in which, he told me, he never could have a fire, for all the smoke came out into the room. I flattered myself I could easily find the cause, and prescribe the cure. I had a fire made there, and found it as he said. I opened the door, and perceived it was not want of air. I made a temporary contraction of the opening of the chimney, and found that it was not its being too large, that caused the smoke to issue. I went out and looked up at the top of the chimney; its funnel was joined in the same stack with others, some of them shorter, that drew very well, and I saw nothing to prevent its doing the same. In fine, after every other examination I could think of, I was obliged to own the insufficiency of my skill. But my friend, who made no pretension to such kind of knowledge, afterward discovered the cause himself. He got to the top of the funnel by a ladder, and looking down, found it filled with twigs and straw cemented by earth, and lined with feathers. . . . The rubbish, considerable in quantity, being removed, and the funnel cleared, the chimney drew well, and gave satisfaction.

8. Buying a Wood-Burning Stove

Traditionally, there are two major purchases the average American makes in his lifetime, his house and his car; with the mobile corporate employee, and with the obsolescence factor built into today's automobiles, this is no longer nearly so true. It may well be that the most critical purchase in time to come will be a wood-burning stove; not because of its cost, but because of the importance of its contribution to the comfort of daily living. Fortunately, not even the most expensive wood-burning stove costs so much that you cannot replace it if you feel you have made a mistake on your first purchase; but you might spend a few uncomfortable and frustrating winters in the meantime.

Because of the variables involved—both in stoves and in people—it is impossible to give you an exact blueprint to follow in making your first purchase. There are, however, several factors to consider, and you might want to use them as a checklist when stove shopping.

AREA TO BE HEATED

This is obviously of first consideration—and it is not just a matter of a simple measurement (although that comes first).

Cubic Feet

Measure it—a guess can be surprisingly far off. If you don't know how, ask your dealer.

Heat-Reducing Features

Note wall-to-wall windows, number of conventional windows, unusually high ceilings (anything over the standard eight feet), slate floors.

Floor Base

Is the area over an unfinished cellar, a finished cellar, or crawl space?

Floor Plan

If you intend to heat more than one room, do a rough sketch of your floor plan; some floor plans have a good pattern for getting the heat from one room to another—some are almost impossible to heat with one stove even if the overall cubic foot measurement is moderate.

Type of House

Since heat rises, a two-story house is easier to heat than a ranch or one-story type; this is true even with ordinary central heating. If you are building a house and economy is a factor, a two-story house is a better buy; not only heating, but plumbing and other costs are less in the conventional two-story than in the conventional ranch. It also makes better use of your land, leaving more room for a garden or outdoor recreation area.

If you already have a ranch, you may need two stoves to heat an area that

A page of stoves offered by Sears, Roebuck and Co., 1897.

BOX SUNSHINE.
Eight sizes, Nos. 18, 22, 25, 28, 30, 35, 37, 42.
A new wood Box Stove.

No. 15888.

No. 15888. A handsome, durable heavy stove. The sides of the three largest sizes are made in two sections to prevent cracking.

No. 18, with one 6-inch boiler hole, 55 lbs.................................$ 2.58
No. 22, with one 7-inch boiler hole, 75 lbs................................. 3.48
No. 25, with two 7-inch boiler holes, 100 lbs............................. 4.20
No. 28, with two 8-inch boiler holes, 125 lbs............................. 5.40
No. 30, with two 8-inch boiler holes, 130 lbs............................. 5.88
No. 35, with two 9-inch boiler holes, 180 lbs............................. 7.50
No. 37, with two 9-inch boiler holes, 190 lbs............................. 8.10
No. 42, with two 9-inch boiler holes, 260 lbs.............................12.90

HEATING STOVES.
Elwood.

No. 15889. The Elwood Heating Stoves, for wood only, a well made stove, mounted with sheet iron body. Has full nickeled foot rail and two cooking holes under swing top.

Size.	Length of fire chamber.	Height.	Weight.	Price.
19	19 in.	45 in.	87 lbs.	$6.00
22	22 in.	47 in.	105 lbs.	7.20
25	25 in.	49 in.	134 lbs.	8.40

No. 15889.

DUKE CANNON STOVE.
For hard or soft coal.

No. 15895. Four sizes. The Duke is the best and most complete cannon stove of its class in the market. It is a powerful heater at a very low price. It has a swing feed door and the top is arranged so that a drum can be attached if desired.

No.	Diameter of fire pot.	Weight.	Height.	Price.
3	8½ in.	35 lbs.	22 in.	$2.40
4	9½ in.	48 "	24 in.	2.70
5	10½ in.	55 "	27 in.	3.48
6	12 in.	70 "	30 in.	3.90

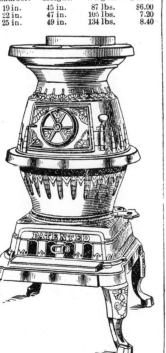

No. 15895.

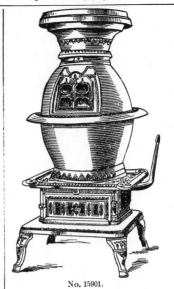

No. 15901.

RADIANT SUNSHINE.

No. 15908. The Radiant Sunshine is the most beautiful, as well as the most complete and practical, of all the round fire pot Franklin stoves in the market. By closing the upper sliding mica doors, the stove can be used as an air-tight surface burner. These doors are so made that they never warp or stick. An efficient dust-flue carries away into the draft all the dust produced by cleaning the fire.

The center discharge grate as applied in this stove is unexcelled for effectiveness and convenience.

The design and ornamentation of the Radiant Sunshine are highly artistic. The skirt base, foot rail, dome plate and swing cover are nickel plated and the appearance of the stove is further enriched by six specially designed circular art tiles.

No.	Size of fire pot.	Weight.	Price.
24	12 in.	147 lbs.	$12.60
28	14 in.	171 lbs.	13.30
32	16 in.	205 lbs.	14.85

GLOBE LIGHTHOUSE.
For hard or soft coal.

No. 15901. Four sizes, with plain grates. A strictly first-class Globe Stove of large size, adapted for bituminous or anthracite coal. The arrangement of the top permits a sheet iron section to be added without additional castings. It is provided with a clinkerless center discharge grate.

No.	Weight.	Height.	Price.
113	189 lbs.	42 in.	$ 6.60
115	170 lbs.	46 in.	8.40
117	220 lbs.	50 in.	10.50
120	307 lbs.	54 in.	14.10

No. 15908.

THE OAK SUNSHINE.
For hard or soft coal or wood.

No. 15912. With hard or soft coal fixture.
No. 15913. With wood fixture.
No. 15914. With both fixtures, add $1.00 to prices quoted.

This cut represents the finest and best "Oak" Stove yet made. Made of first-class material. Thoroughly mounted. Elaborately ornamented. It has full nickeled skirting and nickeled swing dome, an elegant and expensive urn, nickeled and tile door ornaments, nickel foot rails, nickel name plate, two check dampers in feed doors and one in collar. Vibrating grate with draw center, and sheet iron ash pan.

No.	Weight.	Height.	Price.
113	145 lbs.	47 in.	$ 8.10
115	168 lbs.	52 in.	9.60
117	194 lbs.	56 in.	11.40
119	230 lbs.	60 in.	13.55
119½	245 lbs.	72 in.	16.20

No. 15912.

would normally require one. However, you are already paying more for heat so the saving in switching to wood will still be in proportion.

TEMPERATURE WANTED

Americans are known around the world for their overheated houses. By English standards, for example, we live in a perpetual hothouse atmosphere all winter. Since the time of the fuel shortage, many of us have become accustomed to seventy-degree settings and feel fairly comfortable as long as that is maintained. At night we may turn the thermostat down to sixty or sixty-five degrees; we seldom settle for less.

If this is what you require, discuss it with your dealer. It is unlikely that you will be able to maintain this level of heat throughout the entire house; bathrooms, especially, with their expanse of tile, tend to be cooler than other rooms.

However, a cooler temperature is much better for you, and it is largely a matter of getting used to it. Also, if you are cutting your own wood, your own interior heating system is going to be more efficient than it has been since you were a kid, and you'll find you feel hot when everyone else is reaching for an extra sweater.

Don't misunderstand me—you can make the house as hot as you want it with wood-burning stoves, but since you are changing your life-style anyway, why not improve your health at the same time by trying to live a little cooler.

SUPPLEMENTAL OR FULL-SCALE HEATING

If you already have central heating, don't plan to completely replace it unless you have had previous experience with wood-burning stoves. People have cut their heating and cooking bills enormously just by using a wood-burning stove to supplement their regular heating system.

For instance, if you have electric heat with a thermostat in every room, you can turn the thermostat down very low in the room in which you have the stove, and leave the bathroom thermostats at a higher setting. Since the stove will probably be in your most lived-in room, that room will probably also be your largest; you can save a considerable amount of fuel by not using your central heating much in that area.

PLACEMENT AND VENTING

All manufacturers will provide installation instructions with their stoves and you should follow them exactly. But it is helpful to be able to tell the dealer whether you plan to vent the stove into an already existing fireplace, into an unbroken wall, or through the ceiling and attic to the roof. He will be able to advise you, for instance, whether the stove you are considering may be able to heat the second floor by venting up through it; or even whether you want to put the stove in the basement (not generally advisable unless you are installing a furnace).

If you have hot-air ducts, you might be able to utilize them to create a flow of hot air throughout the various rooms and from one floor to another; discuss this at length with your dealer and do not allow an excess of optimism to lead you into an unhappy heating arrangement.

Remember, installation costs money and your dealer can't estimate this cost unless he has a clear picture of what is involved.

FUNCTION OF YOUR STOVE

Here again we come to the question of whether you are planning to use wood-burning stoves only, or merely to supplement your central heating system. This is a critical decision, especially if you are planning to switch over entirely to a wood-burning stove. I urge you not to do so unless you have visited and talked to people who have already done it, or unless you, personally, have had considerable experience with heating with wood.

For complete reliance on wood-burning, you obviously need a stove of the size and efficiency to keep you comfortable and to keep your pipes from freezing in even the most distant rooms. The dealer should come to your home and look at the situation at first hand; in case of an error in planning, you can always bundle up temporarily, but there is nothing quick and simple you can do about your water pipes.

AVAILABILITY OF WOOD

If you have a source for free or very inexpensive wood, you don't have to be so concerned with how fast the stove burns wood. If you think you may have to buy most of your wood, balance the cost of the stove against how efficiently it burns wood; it may be that a more expensive stove will soon pay for itself in that it may require much less wood to produce the same amount of heat as an inexpensive stove.

AVAILABILITY OF LABOR

If you work at home and can keep an eye on the stove, you can buy one that is less efficient in terms of holding a fire, or one that has a smaller firebox and needs to be fed oftener.

If you are away part of the day and want to come home to a moderately warm house and a banked fire, you need a stove that will hold the live coals and heat for that length of time. This may influence your choice between a thermostatically controlled stove and one that is not.

PRICE

Stoves can be had in a very wide range of prices. Although you do not always get what you pay for, and although you may be paying for features you do not want or need, it is often true that the more expensive stoves have more to offer. The first step is to understand *why* a stove is more expensive; if it's merely because of a fancier trim, you may well decide to do without it.

The inexpensive stoves may supply your needs adequately and give you valuable experience in managing a wood-burning stove (a thermostatically controlled stove may not, because it does some of the work for you). Inexpensive stoves will still save a lot of money over last year's heating bill.

Also, no matter how much you may prefer the expensive stoves, you may not be able to afford the initial outlay at this time.

It is still better to buy the best you can afford—so long as you realize that price is not invariably synonymous with quality. Forgo some of the more

sophisticated devices and designs; concentrate first on good materials, a tightly fitting door (or doors), and well-sealed plates. If you are still under your price, see what real advantages you can move up to, baffles, heat exchangers, and so on.

Be sure to check what the price includes. As with automobiles, a number of necessary features may be listed as accessories and cost you extra. If you have to pay extra for a radio in a car, you can do without it; but if one of the optional accessories is a heater, you know you have to add its cost to the price of the car.

The same is true of stoves; some manufacturers include everything—and a few extras—in their base price; some offer a stripped-down product that won't really function at full efficiency without some "optional" equipment. As consumers we are all conditioned to the idea that optional means it costs extra, and we have pretty much forgotten that its real definition is "involving an option—*not compulsory*." Perhaps someday some consumer group will crack down on the casual use of optional to describe necessities that have to be paid for separately from the main purchase.

UPKEEP

If you are the kind of person who oils his tools when they aren't going to be used for a while, and carefully drains his lawnmower motor in November, you won't be concerned if you have to stove-black or paint your cast-iron stove once a year. However, if you never have time for household chores, you won't want to add to them. In this case, think twice about cast iron (unless it is enameled); it will rust unless you take care of it.

On the other hand, maybe you shouldn't let upkeep influence your decision. Stove-blacking isn't a particularly arduous task, and it's little enough to do for a stove that is keeping you warm and comfortable nine months of the year.

AVAILABILITY OF PARTS

Just as with automobiles, some manufacturers are more reliable than others when it comes to replacing parts. You have to assume that some time or other you will need replacements. Ask around to find out what experience your dealer or local wood-stove owners have had with various brands. The dealer may not want to volunteer information, but if you raise the question, he may admit that one manufacturer has a better reputation in that area than another. Ashley, for example, has been in continuous production since 1905, and Mr. Staba of The Colonial Stove Shoppe in Higganum, Connecticut, told me very proudly that he had been able to get parts for Ashleys that were over forty years old and still in use by some of his customers. This is equally true of other good manufacturers—including some that have been in production only a couple of years. But it is a legitimate question to ask, and you should

Contemporary wood-burning kitchen range in home in Wilton, Connecticut. Photo by Marj Loeper.

make a point of it. At the very least, if the dealer has told you parts are readily available and then doesn't deliver, you can give him a really hard time.

COMBINATION STOVES

At present coal is very expensive—when you can get it. There seems to be no reason why wood shouldn't continue to be our most inexpensive and practical fuel. However, as wood stoves become more popular, there is no doubt that dealers will try to escalate the cost of a cord of wood. For this reason, if you have to buy wood, you may want to get a stove that can burn either wood or coal—or be easily adapted to coal—so that you can, temporarily, turn to coal if wood prices threaten to get out of hand. There is no use getting away from the high cost of public utilities only to find yourself at the mercy of your local wood dealer.

MATERIALS

Here we enter a very controversial area; proponents of cast iron will tell you sheet metal is no good at any gauge; sheet-metal fanciers will dismiss cast iron and say sheet metal is great as long as you keep away from the very thin gauge stoves, which they slightingly refer to as "tin" stoves. Actually, there are advantages and disadvantages to both these materials.

Cast Iron

Weight. Cast iron is heavy. Once you get a stove into place, this may not be a disadvantage, but it certainly isn't very portable.

Brittleness. Cast iron cracks easily; it can be broken with a sharp blow from a stove rake or shovel, or by banging it against something while setting it in place.

Seasoning. As you already know if you have used cast-iron frying pans, it must be "seasoned" or "broken-in" by building a dozen or so moderate fires in the beginning. If you build too big a fire in a cast-iron stove at any time, it may crack it.

Upkeep. As we've already mentioned, most cast iron needs to be stove-blackened or painted at least once a year.

Thermo-sensitivity. Cast iron is very sensitive to temperature changes. If you bring in an icy or snow-covered log from outdoors, do not lean it against the stove or put it on the fire until it has thawed out and warmed up a little. Anything too cold in contact with the stove will crack it.

As long as you treat your cast-iron stove with respect, however, it will give you generations of service; most of the antique stoves around are cast iron (though many of them are cracked).

Cast iron is also very good at holding heat, once it has warmed up. It makes a great surface for cooking; the Defiant, for instance, makes the most of this feature with a special griddle cooktop that is removable for cleaning but can be used for making griddle cakes and similar grilled foods right on the stove top. No one who has used cast iron for cooking needs to be told about this, and you are in for a pleasant surprise if you have never experienced the speed and flavor with which foods cook on cast iron.

Sheet Metal, Low-Carbon Steel, and Other Metals

The terminology of stove metals other than cast iron is confusing. For instance, David Squires, of Better 'n Ben's stoves, said one of the reasons his stoves perform much better than similar stoves is that they are made of low-carbon steel (also called black iron), which is not a rolled steel. Low-carbon steel has three times the tensile strength of cast iron and a higher melting point. Mr. Squires was quick to point out that this last factor isn't really important because both have such a high melting point that both are suitable stove material in this regard. However, he emphasized that the low-carbon steel he uses is 11-gauge as compared with the 14-gauge of some much more expensive stoves. Since even 14-gauge is good, it would seem that his stoves are exceptionally sturdy.

In trying to wade through the forest of names for the metals of stoves other than cast iron, try to check other factors that you *can* compare. If you narrow your choice down to one or two, do not hesitate to talk to the dealer or distributor in your area and ask him why his stove is better than the others you are considering. You will usually get an honest answer—even if it is only that his stove is better looking but he can't say, in all fairness, that it will perform any better.

Weight. Sheet metal is lighter than cast iron. If you want to put a stove away for the summer or move it into an obscure corner, it's easier with a sheet-metal stove simply because of its lighter weight.

Thinness. Because sheet metal isn't as thick as cast iron, it is more liable to "burn through" and should be checked at the beginning of every season for thin spots. However, if you don't burn your fires too hot—and you shouldn't in any stove, regardless of material—this won't happen very easily.

Gauge. This is the single most important thing to be aware of in looking at sheet-metal stoves. The number of the gauge indicates how thick the metal has been rolled; *the lower the number, the thicker the metal.* For example, 12-gauge sheet metal is stronger and thicker than 18-gauge.

So-called "tin" stoves indicate that they are made from a very light gauge; "blued steel" generally refers to a light gauge.

In good stoves, different parts of the stove will be made of heavier gauges, as required. For instance, the United States Stove makes a Franklin which is a combination of cast iron and plate steel. They call their steel "plate steel" to differentiate it as much as possible from thin sheet metal. Their firebox is 12-gauge, the hearth 10-gauge, and the main top 8-gauge. Mr. Rodger Castleberry of United States Stove Company wrote me concerning this matter:

The benefit of the steel in these functional parts is, of course, its inherent strength, resistance to cracking and burning out. Some wood stoves have given steel stoves a bad name because of engineering mistakes, primarily in the area of failure to provide deep embossments in the steel itself to deter any consequent warping. Ours, on the other hand, are heavily embossed and resist warping even under the hottest fires.

Sheet metal goes by many names in an effort to avoid the bad connotations it has acquired through the use of thin gauges. Russia steel, for instance, was often used in the 1800s because Russia sheet iron was highly regarded, and sheet-metal stove makers drew some luster from implying that their stoves were made of this material.

Do not dismiss a stove because it is made of sheet metal; it has advantages and disadvantages—and it would not be used by so many excellent and reputable stove manufacturers if it were not a good material. You will bless it every cold morning you rise in the winter for the fact that it will heat up much more quickly than your neighbor's cast iron. (Although he, on the other hand, will bask in heat long after your sheet-metal stove has cooled down.)

WEIGHT

A good rule of thumb for judging the quality of a stove is weight; generally speaking, the heavier the stove, the better it is. However, like all flat statements, this requires certain qualifications.

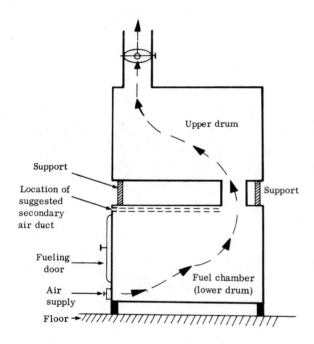

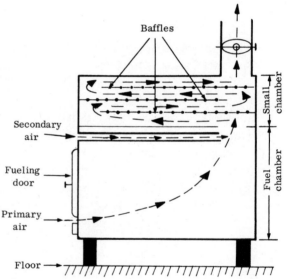

Left: *Oil drums can be used to make a stove. Vertical section through a logging camp stove built of two oil drums mounted one above the other.* Right: *Vertical section through a suggested modification of logging camp stove shown at left. From* Wood as a Home Fuel, *Cooperative Extension Services of the Northeast States.*

Stoves must be *comparable in size*. It's no trick for a larger stove to weigh more than a smaller one.

Stoves must be *made of the same materials;* it's not fair to compare the weight of a cast-iron stove to a sheet-metal one. Even a poor-quality cast-iron stove will usually weigh more than a top-quality sheet-metal one.

Be sure weights are expressed in comparable terms. Some weights are shipping weights—which usually means they include the crate and so on; some include the cabinet, which is a decorative rather than a functional feature and not particularly valid as a basis of comparison. So check out your weights, but be sure you know what is being weighed.

SUMMARY

Even if you can't check out all the above information and factors, at least ask questions. You're not supposed to be the expert; the dealer is. And don't settle for a look at one or two stoves unless you have a great deal of faith in your retailer; there are different stoves for different people and different situations. If you don't have a good selection to choose from, how can you make an intelligent choice?

It may seem like a lot of trouble to go to just to buy a stove, but there are more differences among wood-burning stoves than there are among refrigerators, automobiles, and other purchases you may be accustomed to making; and these differences can mean a comfortable or a miserably chilly winter.

To help you learn about what is available, I have researched a number of stoves offered by manufacturers both here and abroad and have tried to give you some of the basic specifications and claims for each (see Chapter 10). Do not hesitate to take this book with you when you go shopping, and to ask your dealer about any stoves described here that seem right for you.

9. the Wood-Burner's Glossary

These definitions are strictly from the point of view of wood burning and are not meant to be for use outside of this area. They are meant to help you to understand manufacturers' material, store dealers' explanations, and government bulletins—and the somewhat specialized field of heating with wood.

AIR-DRY   A term applied to wood that has been dried under normal, reasonably sunny outdoor conditions. Air-dried wood is presumed to contain about 20 percent moisture.

BAFFLE   A device, such as a plate, a series of channels, or a wall to deflect or regulate the flow of volatiles from the fire to the flue in order to obtain more complete combustion or retain heat longer within the stove.

BTU   British thermal unit, or the amount of heat required to raise the temperature of one pound of water one degree Fahrenheit.

BUCK   To cut wood to length desired.

CAST IRON   An alloy of iron, carbon, and silicon that is cast in a mold. By nature it is extremely durable but brittle and can be cracked by a sharp blow or excessive heat.

CHAIN SAW   A portable power saw with teeth linked together to form an endless chain that goes around in an oval. It is powered by a simple gasoline motor.

CHUNK   A short thick piece of wood, often waste wood.

CORD   A stack of cut wood 4 by 4 by 8 feet (128 cubic feet). A cord of hardwood weighs approximately two tons. See also *face cord*.

CREOSOTE   A tarlike substance resulting from the distillation of wood during combustion; as volatiles pass through the chimney flue, they cool and are deposited on the flue walls rather than being vented out the chimney into the air. There is some disagreement as to whether creosote is actually inflammable; it is agreed, however, that it is an undesirable deposit, and its formation is to be avoided whenever possible. It can also form on stovepipes, dampers, and any other object between the fire and the outdoor air, whenever the temperature in that area drops below 250 degrees Fahrenheit.

CUBIC FEET   Area to be heated is often expressed in terms of cubic feet, which is determined by multiplying the height times width times length of your area. Some manufacturers prefer to describe their stoves in terms of number of rooms heated because they feel that gives a more graphic picture to the average homeowner. There is no doubt that a stove that will heat ten rooms sounds very efficient; whereas "cubic feet" does not mean very much, in the beginning, to the average consumer.

Since, in any case, this type of measurement is only a rough guide, you will soon learn to compare area heated no matter how it is expressed.

DAMPER   A valve or plate that regulates the draft, usually located in the stovepipe or chimney. Manufacturers of airtight stoves generally do not recommend the use of dampers with their stoves. Most other stoves require them for efficient draft control.

DRAFT CONTROL   A way of letting in or closing off air to the interior of the stove. The rate at which fire burns depends on how much air is let into the firebox; whether the air is prewarmed, let in at top or bottom, and so on, also affect burning efficiency, but an ample supply of oxygen is the first requirement.

Draft controls can be simple or highly sophisticated; study diagrams where they are available so as to familiarize yourself with the various plans—you may be able to invent something even better than present-day systems.

ENAMEL   An opaque vitreous compound applied by fusion to the surface of metal. Stoves with an enamel finish are easy to maintain because they do not need to be painted or blackened.

FACE CORD   A stack of wood 4 feet by 8 feet by 16 inches or shorter, equal to about one-third of a standard cord. Also known as a "run" or "rick."

FIREBRICK   A brick made of a special clay so that it can withstand a high degree of heat—more than 2,700 degrees Fahrenheit. They are used for lining fireplaces, furnaces, some stoves, and stove bottoms. They will not crumble in heat as will ordinary bricks.

FIRE CLAY   A fine clay used where exposure to high temperatures requires the ability to withstand heat without breaking down. Some fire clays will withstand temperatures as high as 3,500 degrees Fahrenheit. Ideally, firebricks should be mortared with fire clay (as well as made of it).

Not all so-called fire clays are of this quality, and the reputation of the brand or of your bricklayer is your only assurance that you are getting the product your conditions require.

FLUE   A channel in a chimney for conveying flame and smoke to the outer air.

GASKET   Packing to make a joint or door airtight. Gaskets may be made of metal, rubber, or asbestos; most wood-burning–stove gaskets are made of asbestos.

GAUGE   The measure of the thickness of a material—such as sheet metal. In sheet metal the lower the gauge number, the thicker the metal.

HARDWOOD   The dictionary definition isn't much help here. It says: "a tree that yields hardwood." In general, hardwood trees are denser, drier, and nonresinous, such as oak, hickory, locust. Pines and other conifers are not hardwood. Hardwood is considered more desirable as fuel.

HEAT EXCHANGER   Usually another heat chamber on top of the part that holds the firebox. Volatiles go from the firebox, are baffled around the chamber, and then vented to the stovepipe. It increases the area from which heat is radiated into the room and increases materially the amount of heat that is given off by the fire.

INSULATION   Insulation is what keeps the heat in and the cold out; whether it is glass fiber blown between the walls or blanketlike insulation strips. This is just as important in wood-heated homes as in other types of heating.

A home that has been insulated for electric heat will give you the best results because it is the best insulated; a house that is poorly built with thin walls will be harder to warm and to keep warm. If you don't think you are getting the heat you should from your stove, check out your insulation.

KINDLING   Small twigs and thin pieces of wood that are easily combustible so that they will catch fire quickly when lit. Resinous woods, such as pine and other softwoods, which might not be desirable as regular firewood, make excellent kindling.

LOG-SPLITTER   A mechanical device for splitting wood. Log-splitters come in all price ranges, and if you are splitting your own wood, you would be well advised to invest in one. If you are splitting a lot of wood, you might want to get together with your neighbors and buy one of the more expensive ones that run on a gasoline motor.

OVEN WOOD   Wood that has been split into fairly short, thin pieces and then air-dried. It is sometimes even kept within the house for a week or two. It is used primarily for cookstoves to create fast, high heat. In colonial days it was used within the wall ovens to build the fires that heated them to proper baking temperatures.

SHEET METAL Metal in the form of a sheet.

SOFTWOOD Generally speaking, resinous woods such as pines. Resinous woods burn hard and fast. Softwoods are lighter in weight than hardwoods and not as good a buy; if you are buying by the cord, you will get more heat for your money out of a cord of hardwood.

SOOT A fine, black, powdery substance formed by chemical breakdown in the combustion of wood. It may adhere to stovepipes, dampers, chimneys, and other surfaces, much in the manner of creosote, and is considered highly inflammable. It is very important not to allow soot build-up.

STOVE A portable or fixed apparatus that burns fuel or uses electricity to provide heat for cooking and heating.

STOVEPIPE A pipe of large diameter, usually of sheet metal used as a stove chimney or to connect a stove with a flue.

THERMOSTATICALLY CONTROLLED The term describing a stove which has an automatic device, usually bimetallic, which is activated by temperature to open or close the draft.

UNIT A stack of 16-inch wood, 2 feet by 2 feet. Usually—due to the weight of wood—the most a station wagon can carry.

VOLATILES An umbrella term for the gases given off by wood when it begins to break down chemically in the presence of heat; technically wood does not burn—it is the volatiles and the charcoals formed by wood that actually burn.

10. the Wood-Burning Stove Catalog

OAK SUNSHINE

HOW TO USE THIS CATALOG

No single dealer—no matter how extensive his stock of stoves—will be able to show you all the stoves described in this catalog. He will have bought the ones he thinks will sell well in his area, and sometimes his choice may not include the stove that is best for you. This catalog provides a much larger view of wood-burning stoves, offering a wide selection; it acquaints you with some fine but less well-known stoves, as well as with the heavily advertised and widely distributed ones.

You can survey the field at home at your leisure, make notes, raise questions, talk it over with your family, and go to your dealer much better equipped than the average wood-stove purchaser, who is unfamiliar with what is available, or knows only the one or two stoves that his friends and acquaintances have used.

Of course, space limitations, as well as a rapidly expanding market, make it impossible to include every good wood-burning stove made. This catalog offers a representative group in each of the most important categories: Franklin stoves, Scandinavian stoves, cookstoves and ranges, furnaces, and so on.

At the end of the catalog, there is a list of the names and addresses of manufacturers and importers, divided into these same categories, listed alphabetically under the names of the stoves they represent. To find the name and address, simply look under the proper category for the name of the stove. If a manufacturer precedes the name of the stoves with his own name, as Lange 6302K, Lange 6203BR, etc., there will only be one listing, "Lange," under that category.

You will find the list includes both stoves described and illustrated in the catalog and additional manufacturers not so described. In all cases, feel free to write for more information about any stoves that interest you; you will find everyone in the field very helpful.

Specifications

Ideally, specifications are most useful if presented in a uniform way. Since this is impossible, I have used the manufacturers' specifications.

For instance, sometimes the heating capacity is given in terms of number of rooms heated, sometimes in cubic feet, rarely in terms of Btu's. If the consumer knew how to interpret the figures, Btu's would probably be the most accurate measure, but many manufacturers feel that number of rooms is more meaningful and graphic to the consumer.

Since conditions under which a stove will be used vary so greatly, no one measurement tells the whole story of what stove will heat your home effectively. Use the heating capacity figures as a general guide to the amount of heat produced.

Descriptions

All claims ("the greatest," and so on) and all facts, such as specifications, have been gleaned either from manufacturers' and importers' printed material or in the course of extended conversations and interviews with them. In no case does it represent a value judgment or endorsement. Read the descriptions and specifications with the same reservations you would apply in reading any advertising material.

Graphics

Not all photographs and other material furnished by manufacturers are of equal quality—that doesn't mean their stoves aren't. Americans are used to graphically sophisticated presentations—packaging, photographs, well-drawn diagrams, and so on. Many of the older, time-tested manufacturers are making a product that has been selling itself for many, many years; sometimes their graphics have not caught up with the times. Do not be put off by an apparently unattractive product. Ask yourself, if it's so unattractive, how come it's still selling? It must have something going for it. This isn't invariably the case, but it's worth consideration.

Prices

I cannot emphasize too strongly that the prices given here may now be out-of-date. They are included as a basis for *comparison,* and as a guide to *price range.* In other words, if you have only $100 to spend on a stove, the prices indicated will keep you from wasting your time shopping for a $600 one. However, the $100 may be $125 or even $150 by the time you go shopping.

Heating Capacities

Some manufacturers are somewhat optimistic about the heating capacity of their units; some lean over backward to give a lower figure than they believe is actually the case, so that a margin is left for less than optimum conditions. For instance, they don't like to use the maximum figure because they know that most homes are not perfectly insulated, draft free, with ideal chimneys in a windless, sheltered site. They would rather have you pleasantly surprised by how well the stove heats, than disappointed in how it performs in your home.

If the difference between two stoves you are considering is critical to you, consult with the dealer. It is also possible to get from him the names of people who have already used those stoves through a season and can tell you firsthand what their experiences have been. Here, again, however, you will have to know what you are looking at, and whether the stoves have been used under conditions comparable to yours.

Go to the Source

If you cannot decide between two stoves that seem to be very similar, write to the manufacturers. Describe the two stoves you are considering, your circumstances and heating requirements, and ask each one why his stove would be better for your purposes than his competitor's.

It's okay to ask the dealer first, if he seems knowledgeable—but if you are not satisfied with his answer, go right to the source.

It may be, of course, that both stoves are equally satisfactory, and it may be awkward for anyone to tell you so. If that seems to be the case, don't press. Decide on the basis of which appeals to you more in terms of appearance and so forth.

In comparing prices, be sure you are talking about comparable things. Does the price include everything you will need to install and run the stove—fire screens and other necessary accessories? Is stovepipe included? Are the stoves equally easy to install or will one require a skilled workman?

Talking to Users

Do not rush out and buy a stove on the advice of one person using one stove. I have found, in numerous interviews, that most people either love or hate (and I use emotional words on purpose) the stove they are using. This is simply not a rational reaction—on the one hand, you tend to get fond of something you take care of; on the other hand, some people just cannot get the hang of one stove and can manage another very well. If you are seeking a consumer's advice, ask more than one consumer about more than one stove.

SUMMARY

Many of the manufacturers neglect to include useful information—just because it isn't mentioned, do not assume it doesn't exist. For instance, most stoves carry some sort of guarantee, but it isn't always clearly noted; do not hesitate to ask about it, and about anything you want to know but cannot find listed.

Franklin Stoves

BEN FRANKLIN

Manufactured by the King Stove & Range Company, the Ben Franklin can be used with wood, coal, charcoal, or gas-fired logs. It is handsomely designed with colonial motifs, made of cast iron, like the original Franklin.

Two sizes are available: the 98-1800, which weighs 300 lbs.; and the 98-1830, which weighs 385 lbs. Specifications are given for the smaller stove.

Specifications 98-1800

Dimensions: 29½" high x 26" deep
　　　　　　Width at front:　37"
　　　　　　Width at rear:　24"
Price: Approximately $299.95
Material: Cast iron
Weight: 300 lbs.
Optional equipment: Fire screen, barbecue grill, bean pot, swing-out hanger, and many other items

ATLANTA FRANKLIN FIREPLACE STOVE 32

Atlanta offers Franklin stoves in three sizes, from large free-standing models to a small, low model that will fit into the fireplace.

All stoves are sturdily built of cast iron with a basket-type grate that allows the stove to be used for wood, coal, or charcoal. An easy-to-reach damper on the vent allows you to control the draft so that you can have a blazing fire or glowing coals. As with all Franklins, the stove can be operated open to view the fire or closed for maximum heating; a fire screen is available as an option.

The stove is adapted to fireplace accessories offered by Atlanta that allow cooking over the open fire; these include a swing-out bean pot for stews, soups, and similar dishes, and a swing-out grill for broiling that adjusts to six different cooking levels.

Specifications

For #32 only

Dimensions: 41½" high x 44"wide x 30" deep

Flue size: 10"

Firebox size: 32" front width
26" rear width
19¾" high

Material: Cast iron

Shipping weight: 400 lbs.

THE EAGLE FRANKLIN

The Eagle Franklin is made by the Portland Stove Foundry of Portland, Maine, which has been in continuous production since 1877. It has draft-control slides on both doors, which fold for viewing of the open fire; there is a baffle plate to minimize heat loss.

A number of options are available in both cast iron and solid brass; the solid brass eagles shown in the photograph are an example.

The construction is solid cast iron, and the design is based on patterns from 1742 plates. In addition to the Eagle, the Portland Stove Foundry makes six other Franklin stoves.

Specifications

Dimensions: Width of front at top: 35¾″
Width of hearth: 39⅝″
Height, floor to top: 32½″
Depth, hearth to front: 11¼″
Width of back, inside: 21⅜″
Width of front
  opening: 27¼″
Smoke pipe size: 8″

Price: Approximately $433, not including options
Material: Cast iron
Weight: 300 lbs.
Options available: Many, including grills, grates, spark guards, heat shields, cranes, bean pots, fenders, and so on; in cast iron or solid brass
Guarantee: Unconditionally guaranteed for 10 years

JØTUL #4 →

This combination open fireplace and wood stove has a door that ingeniously slides down on hidden iron rails to store out of the way underneath the fireplace; it is balanced so that a slight pull on the handle turns the fireplace back into a cast-iron stove. An adjustable draft vent on the door gives controlled-draft, front-to-back burning, typical of Scandinavian stoves. Fire screen is provided for safety in viewing the open fire.

Specifications

Made in Norway
Dimensions: 41.3″ high x 22.6″ wide x 22.4″ long
Firebox size: Holds 14″ logs
Height to lower edge of flue pipe: 30.1″
Stovepipe size: 7″
Colors and prices: Black or dark green enamel: approximately $620
Materials: Cast iron
Shipping weight: 286 lbs.
Heating capacity: 9,500 cubic feet maximum

LANGE #61MF

A combination open fireplace and stove, from Denmark.

With the doors closed, it operates as an effective heating stove, complete with efficient internal baffle and chimney damper for draft control. Unlike most Franklin fireplaces, the fire can be viewed even when the doors are closed; there is glass in the doors for this purpose. With the doors open, you have an open fireplace.

You can lift off the entire front of the stove and replace it with a screen; this will give you a large view of the open fire.

Specifications

Made in Denmark

Dimensions: 38″ high x 20½″ wide x 19″ deep

Firebox size: 11″ x 14″ minimum; intended for use with tepee fire, 16″ wood

Height to top of flue opening: 37¼″

Stovepipe size: 7″

Colors and prices: Black: approximately $500; red enamel: approximately $620

Materials: Cast iron, with firebox lined with firebrick

Shipping weight: 286 lbs.

Heating capacity: 5,000 to 7,000 cubic feet

◄ *Jøtul #4*

MALM ROYAL FRANKLIN CIRCULATING FIREPLACE

Unlike most Franklin stoves, the hinged "door" is made of glass so that the fire can be viewed equally well with the door open or closed. However, this stove resembles Franklin's original Pennsylvanian Fire-place in that it is double-walled (in this case, sides as well as back), providing cold air intake at the bottom and hot air discharge at the top through side wall ports. A built-in smoke shelf increases draft efficiency.

Specifications

Dimensions: 32″ high x 38″ wide x 23″ deep

Flue size: 8″

Color and price: Black: approximately $325 with glass door, log grate, damper, pipe to 8-foot ceiling

Materials: Heavy 12-gauge steel construction, refractory clay hearth

Shipping weight: 240 lbs.

Optional accessories: Brass ball ornaments, barbecue grill, fire screen

MORSØ 1125

A combination open fireplace and stove, from Denmark.

With doors closed, it operates as an exceptionally efficient stove—increased efficiency, as in the Morsø box stoves, is achieved by a heavy baffle plate above the firebox that holds heat in the stove longer. This model can be either top- or back-vented through the collar, which contains its own spring-loaded damper. Morsø says this has the largest firebox of any cast-iron, airtight, stove-and-fireplace combination on the market.

Two swing-out doors permit full viewing of fire. Doors can be opened, or easily lifted off altogether. Screen is of perforated metal rather than wire mesh to minimize loss of warm air from room—which typically results from the use of any open fireplace.

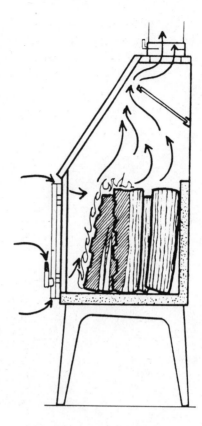

Specifications

Made in Denmark

Dimensions: 41.7″ high x 29.5″ wide x 22.8″ deep

Firebox size: 22″ wide x 17½″ deep; with logs placed horizontally, will take wood lengths up to 20″; with logs placed vertically, up to 16″ long for the back and 20″ long for the front

Flue size: 8″ American

Colors and prices: Black, green, white enamel: approximately $610; red and blue available on special order

Materials: Cast iron, with firebox lined with firebrick

Weight: 310 lbs.

Shipping weight: 354 lbs.

Heating capacity: Approximately 10,000 cubic feet

Guarantee: Unconditionally guaranteed for 1 year

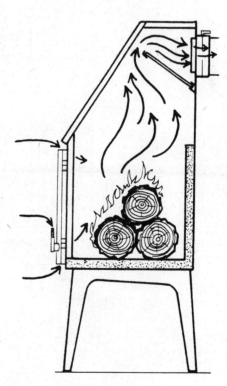

◀ *Morsø 1125*

THE OLYMPIC FRANKLIN

The Olympic Franklin is made by the Washington Stove Works just the way they made it 100 years ago—from the original molds—in the original material, solid cast iron.

The doors fold back against the sides to conserve space when the open fire is viewed, close tightly for greater heat production. The bottom of the stove is one casting, and ashes can be vented into an optional ash drawer.

This Franklin comes in several models, ranging in height (not including legs) from 19⅞ inches to 28⅛ inches, and in price from approximately $255 to $550.

A number of options are available, including a brass finial, brass ball, cast-iron swing-out barbecue grill, brass hearth rail, 3-quart cooking pot with hammered lid, and spark guard screen.

In keeping with Dr. Franklin's own views on the importance of chimneys to a good fire, the informative instruction booklet that accompanies the stove describes and illustrates "twenty causes of chimney troubles and their cures."

THERMO-CONTROL FRANKLIN

The doors of this modern Franklin stove fold back out of the way, flat against the side, leaving a clear view of the open fire behind the triangular fire screen. They close with a graduated locking system.

This stove can be adapted for gas or electric logs; its primary function, however, is wood burning.

Specifications

Dimensions: 28" high x 30" wide x 24" deep

Stovepipe size: 8"

Price: Approximately $219.95; price includes grate and fire screen

Materials: 10-gauge hot-rolled steel, ¼" thick

Weight: 180 lbs.

UNITED STATES STOVE FRANKLIN

A unique combination of cast iron and plate steel. The "aesthetic" parts, such as columns and doors, are cast iron, heavily embossed to deter warping; the functional parts are plate steel, which is used for its inherent strength and resistance to cracking.

This Franklin comes in two models; the smaller one (261-ST) is suitable for use either as a free-standing stove or placed within an existing fireplace. Both models have all the same features and differ only in dimensions and price. They have built-in damper controls and baffles and can be adapted for gas logs.

Cooking can be done in them with the doors open, with the aid of optional equipment.

Specifications 261-ST

Dimensions: Height, with legs: 31¼"
Width top front: 33½"
Width of hearth: 38"
Depth, inside front firebox: 14"
Depth, hearth to front: 13"
Width of back, inside: 20¾"
Width of front opening: 25¾"
Width of top at back: 24¾"

Color and price: Matte black; approximately $199

Material: Cast iron and plate steel
Firebox: 12-gauge
Main top: 8-gauge
Hearth: 10-gauge

Weight: Approximately 230 lbs.

Warranty: 5-year warranty against cracking, warping, or burn-out

Optional accessories: Screen, swing-out barbecue, bean pot, grate, and many, many more items

Scandinavian Stoves

In their class, Scandinavian stoves are considered among the finest made anywhere in the world. All of them are airtight—with the exception of some of the Franklins—are made of cast iron, and bear a family resemblance to one another. However, like members of the human family, there are often considerable differences among them. If this is the kind of stove you think would fit your needs, look at more than one brand before making your choice. This is not difficult, since dealers who carry one Scandinavian stove frequently carry several others.

Although there are differences in the various baffle systems, most Scandinavian box stoves are designed to hold a fire overnight; in fact, their ability to hold a fire for exceptionally long periods of time has led the manufacturers and importers to warn users not to take undue advantage of this feature because it will result in too much creosote and soot buildup. Actually, no wood-burning stove should be allowed to burn for an excessive length of time at the coal stage.

So far as I know, there are no Scandinavian stoves that are thermostatically controlled, but at least one importer feels that that is because they can be managed so efficiently that a thermostat is simply not necessary.

The following section includes a sampling of the models that are available from three of the brands currently being imported. I have not been able to include all importers, and new imports are being introduced every year; so you may find other Scandinavian stoves on the market when you go shopping. At least this group will give you a basis for comparison.

JØTUL 602

The manufacturer calls this cast-iron box stove "Little Giant" because it will heat a medium-sized room in spite of the fact that the 602 is only 19.3 inches long.

Airtight, with baffle and draft-control on the door, this stove has all the sturdy, efficient-combustion features of much larger box stoves. It is also available with decorative top (as shown).

Specifications
Made in Norway

Dimensions: 25.1″ high x 12.8″ wide x
  19.3″ deep
Firebox size: Holds 16″ logs
Height to lower edge of flue pipe: 19.3″
Stovepipe size: 5″
Colors and prices: Black: approximately
  $270; green enamel: approximately
  $300
Materials: Cast iron
Shipping weight: 117 lbs.
Heating capacity: 2,825 to 4,766 cubic
  feet

LANGE 6303A

An especially strong heater with a long firebox and exceptionally large wood capacity for a small stove. Curved side plates add strength and eliminate need for burnplates.

Specifications

Made in Denmark

Dimensions: 23½″ high x 16″ wide x 25″ deep

Firebox size: 20¼″ long

Height to top of flue opening: 25″

Stovepipe size: 5″

Colors and prices: Black: approximately $250 brown; blue, green, red enamel: approximately $295

Materials: Cast iron

Shipping weight: 145 lbs.

Heating capacity: 3,000 to 5,000 cubic feet

MORSØ 6B

A cast-iron box stove that holds an exceptionally large load of wood (16-inch lengths) for its size, with a fully lined firebox. The vertical fluting of the exterior adds 25 percent to the area of side-radiating surfaces.

Because the stove is top loading, it does not require a large hearth to catch the ashes, and ashes can never fall out the front.

The draft control, located on front, has the same type of air-circulator box as in the #2B. Unique baffle system can be seen in accompanying diagram.

Specifications

Made in Denmark
Dimensions: 24.4″ high x 14″ wide x 23.6″ deep
Flue size: 4.7″
Color and prices: Black enamel: approximately $395; price includes ash scoop, two lengths of 18-gauge pipe, elbow, wall thimble, and asbestos rope packing
Materials: Cast iron
Weight: 146 lbs.
Shipping weight: 168 lbs.
Heating capacity: 6,000 cubic feet, approximately

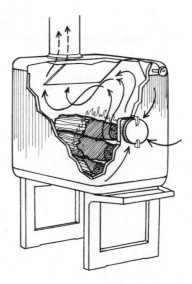

JØTUL 118

Unusual cast-iron stove capable of heating large areas. The embossed Norwegian inscription can be translated as follows: "I built me a flame late one night. When day is done, God will my flame never dies out."

The lid lifts off easily, exposing the baffle which can then be covered with a layer of aluminum foil and used to smoke small quantities of food—according to Jøtul importer Eva Horton, who frequently uses hers for this purpose.

Specifications
Made in Norway
Dimensions: 30.3″ high x 14.2″ wide x 29.5″ deep
Firebox size: Takes 24″ logs
Height to lower edge of flue pipe: 24.6″
Stovepipe size: 5″
Colors and prices: Black: approximately $445; deep green enamel: approximately $500
Materials: Cast iron
Shipping weight: 231 lbs.
Heating capacity: 4,240 to 7,060 cubic feet

LANGE 6203BR

An airtight parlor stove patterned after European tile stoves. The extensive embossing provides a lot of heat in a comparatively small package—good for people who must put a stove in a relatively small space. In spite of its short length, its high heating capacity is indicated by heavy weight and unusually large radiating surface. Has typical, efficient Scandinavian baffle system.

Specifications

Made in Denmark

Dimensions: 41″ high x 13¼″ wide x 20″ deep

Firebox size: 16″ long

Height to top of flue opening: 41″

Stovepipe size: 5″

Colors and prices: Black: approximately $315; brown, blue, green, red enamel: approximately $395

Materials: Cast iron

Shipping weight: 213 lbs.

Heating capacity: 4,000 to 6,000 cubic feet

MORSØ 2B

An airtight, controlled-draft, enameled, cast-iron box stove with draft control on precision-ground, hand-fitted door. Also available with short legs for installing within a masonry fireplace.

Smoke flow pattern and baffle system shown in accompanying diagram.

Specifications

Made in Denmark

Dimensions: 28″ high x 13″ wide x 27½″ deep

Flue size: 4.7″

Colors and prices: Matte black enamel: approximately $315; price includes two pieces of 18-gauge smoke pipe, elbow, wall thimble, stove poker, and sufficient asbestos to seal smoke pipe at thimble

Materials: Cast iron

Weight: 124 lbs.

Shipping weight: 130 lbs.

Heating capacity: 4,800 cubic feet, approximately

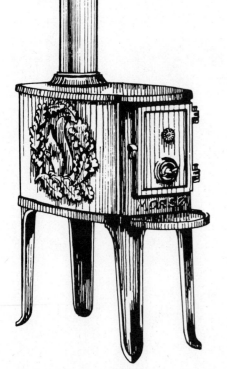

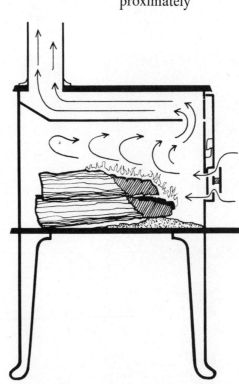

JØTUL 606

Although this stove has the same size firebox as the Jøtul 602, the large heating chamber above the basic box stove plates increases the heating capacity from a maximum of 4,766 cubic feet (for the 602) to a maximum of 7,060 cubic feet (for the 606).

In addition to the extra-large heat chamber, the traditional arch design provides a larger surface area from which heat is radiated.

Specifications

Made in Norway
Dimensions: 41.1" high x 12.4" wide x 19.7" deep
Firebox size: Takes logs 12" long
Height to lower edge of flue pipe: 35"
Stovepipe size: 5"
Color and price: Black; approximately $435
Materials: Cast iron
Shipping weight: 210 lbs.
Heating capacity: 4,240 to 7,060 cubic feet

LANGE 6302K

A handsome airtight box stove for both heating and cooking, this is a powerful heater—good for a big house. Curved, heavy cast-iron plates provide extra strength. Unique baffle system (for extra heat output) can be bypassed for quick-starting fire. The door of each Lange is hand-filed to insure a tight fit.

Second heating chamber contains an oven for baking, with vent for temperature regulation, as well as cooking plate. Firebox has unusually large volume, will hold more fuel in proportion to its length than many other similar stoves. Burn-plates cover entire bottom and inside of stove.

Specifications

Made in Denmark
Dimensions: 50½" high x 16" wide x 34" deep
Firebox length: 26"
Height to top of flue opening: 47¾"
Stovepipe size: 5"
Colors and prices: Black: approx. $595; brown, blue, green, or red enamel: approximately $725
Materials: Cast iron
Shipping weight: 370 lbs.
Heating capacity: 8,000 to 10,000 cubic feet

MORSØ 1BO

An airtight, controlled-draft stove with a graceful heat exchanger arch. The estimated burning time on a full load of dry seasoned hardwood is approximately twelve to sixteen hours.

The smoke flow pattern of the 1BO is similar to the 2BO with one exception: heat flows around both chambers of the arch, meets at the top, and exits through the smoke pipe; there is no restricting baffle in the front chamber. The inward curves of the chamber create a warm air flow upward through the grillwork and out the grilled plates on top.

A box stove model, #1B, without the heat exchanger and with the same baffle system and side linings, is also available.

Specifications

Made in Denmark
Dimensions: 51.2″ high x 14.2″ wide x 30.3″ deep
Firebox size: 22.8″, inside length; 5,186 cubic inches, inside content
Flue collar: 4.7″, inside diameter
Colors and price: Matte black or glossy gray enamel: approximately $640; price includes wall thimble, elbow, 2 pieces of 18-gauge smoke pipe, stove poker, and asbestos packing to seal stovepipe at wall thimble
Materials: Cast iron
Weight: 353 lbs.
Heating capacity: 9,000 cubic feet, approximately

Kitchen Cookstoves and Ranges

ATLANTA COOKSTOVE 8316

Sturdy, well-engineered cookstove, complete with oven and four removable lid tops for placing pots and pans directly over heat source. Manufactured by a company that has been making cookstoves for over eighty-five years.

Specifications

Height to cooking top: 28¾"
Size of top: 30¼" x 21½"
Covers: Four 8" covers
Firebox size: Takes wood up to 17½"
Collar: 6"
Material: Cast iron
Shipping weight: 155 lbs.

ATLANTA 1536 RANGE

This range will burn wood or coal and is capable of maintaining a steady, even temperature that holds for hours and hours. It has well-engineered dampers and draft controls with a handy warming closet and full oven, as well as six removable stove lids that can be taken off (so that pots can be placed directly over the heat for faster cooking).

Also available as a range only, without the warming closet.

Specifications

Height to cooking top: 29½″
Size of top: 35¼″ x 21¼″
Size of oven: 15″ x 14″ x 11″
Covers: Four 8″, two 5½″
Firebox size: Takes wood up to 15″
Collar: 7″
Price: Approximately $436.95
Material: Cast iron
Shipping weight: 285 lbs.

THE QUEEN ATLANTIC RANGE

If you have always wanted a cooking range like the one your great-grand-mother used to have, don't spend time and money hunting for an antique. The Queen Atlantic is probably what you have in mind, and you can buy a brand-new one made in the original foundry from the original patterns—and this is not a reproduction, it is the real thing. The Portland Stove Foundry in Portland, Maine, has been in business since 1877, and this particular range—the Queen Atlantic—has been in continuous production since 1906.

It is built today, as it always has been, of solid cast iron. The outside is available either in natural cast iron, or in an attractive range of colors in porcelain enamel.

The range comes a number of different ways—with or without a warming oven, with or without a water reservoir, and so on. The photograph shows it with a high warming shelf on top; to the right, under an extension of the cooktop, is the water reservoir; to the left of the reservoir is the oven door (with thermometer); to the left of that, the firebox door; and extending out from the left side, a hearth shelf.

The oven with oven thermometer is enormous, designed for the holiday family gatherings come to feast on Grandma's famous cooking. The oven control damper is on top, and the cookstove surface, with removable stove lids, is more than generous.

An extra large and deep firebox holds a large load of fuel and is accompanied by an extra-deep ash pit to minimize work. There is a special flue construction designed for great fuel economy.

In spite of its undoubted appeal as a reminder of the good old days, the Queen Atlantic is an immensely practical range—designed in a no-nonsense way to do the job it is meant for. If its size precludes its use in the modern kitchen, a smaller version—with the same size oven and optional features—is available.

Specifications

Dimensions: 32½″ high x 57″ wide x 30¾″ deep

Firebox size: 23″ long x 9″ wide x 7″ deep

Oven size: 20″ x 20″

Colors and price: Natural cast iron or a choice of colors in porcelain enamel: approximately $1,250

Material: Cast iron

Weight: Approximately 600 lbs.

Guarantee: Unconditionally guaranteed for 10 years.

STANLEY KITCHEN RANGE

The Stanley range is made in Ireland in the town of Waterford, home of Waterford crystal, by a firm that has been furnishing ranges for Irish kitchens for over forty years.

Unlike many wood-burning ranges, the Stanley has a turkey-sized oven, 13 inches high x 15¾ inches wide x 15½ inches deep. Also, unlike most wood-burning ranges, it can be loaded both from the top and from the side—a real convenience if you have pots cooking on the stove top when you need to add wood. Because of this feature, it is possible to burn wood either vertically or horizontally, depending on the size of your logs. The Stanley burns all solid fuels, including wood, for approximately ten hours without attention.

Facing the photograph, the top door on the right is the firebox; the bottom door, the ash pit with spinwheel draft regulator; the large door on the left with the thermometer is the oven. Stove has backsplash and warming shelf.

The stove top has four removable stove lids, but as with all wood-burning cookstoves, cooking can be done anywhere on the top. The oven damper is located in the rear of the cooktop.

In back of the firebox is a glass-lined cast-iron compartment that can be hooked up to a boiler for domestic hot-water production. The firebox itself is airtight.

A handy drying rod in front of the stove provides an old-fashioned feature that modern housewives will appreciate.

Specifications

Made in Ireland

Dimensions: 35⅜″ high x 36″ wide x 21¾″ deep

Oven size: 13″ high x 15¾″ wide x 15½″ deep

Firebox size: Will hold 16″ logs in 17″ firebox in near future; this model holds 12″ logs

Colors and price: White with black porcelain and cast-iron top or matte black finish overall: approximately $499.

Materials: Cast-iron body with glass linings, steel base, sides and rear panels vitreous enamel; firebox is firebrick lined

TIBA KITCHEN RANGE

Made in Switzerland, with characteristically fine Swiss craftsmanship, the Tiba is the product of a firm that specializes in kitchen ranges for homes, hotels, and restaurants.

This model is available in all stainless steel, or in rich shades of blue, green, dark brown, red, or orange enamel. In all models, the cooking surface is cast iron and the remainder of the upper surface stainless steel.

Like most kitchen ranges, the Tiba is top loading. Looking at the photograph, the right-hand part of the cooking surface lifts, with a handle and hinges, to permit fueling. The cooking surface plate can be removed for cleaning, as can the oven.

The main body of the stove is steel, lined with firebrick, which also surrounds the oven and gives the stove unusual mass; once heated, the brick tends to remain hot for a long time, which makes it easier to maintain steady oven temperatures. The stove will continue to give off heat long after the fire in it has died. Dampers are built-in.

The two dials on the right are draft regulators; on the left is the oven thermometer. The upper-right door gives access to a 16-inch firebox, which is brick lined. The lower-right door gives access to the ash drawer. The extensive bottom drawer (the width of the stove) is for storage.

Although not available at present, models which provide domestic hot water and hook into hot-water heating systems will be available in the future.

Specifications

Made in Switzerland

Dimensions: 35″ high x 36″ wide x 24″ deep

Cast-iron cooking surface: 30½″ x 17½″

Firebox size: Just over 16″ long

Oven: 12½″ x 11″ x 17″ deep, with centigrade thermometer

Colors and price: Stainless steel or blue, green, dark brown, red, or orange enamel: approximately $1,000 (stainless slightly higher)

Materials: Stainless steel and steel, firebrick lined; cast-iron cooking surface; firebox firebrick lined

Box Stoves

ATLANTIC BOX STOVE

Atlantic Box Stoves are patterned after a Ford Foundry design of the late nineteenth or early twentieth century. They have been manufactured by the Portland Stove Foundry since 1920, and are hand-cast into sand molds and hand-built.

This is a heavily built stove with a large firebox, which may be side- or top-loaded to fuel maximum-size pieces or chunks of wood. The entire top lifts off for feeding chunks, or the fire can be fueled through the large front door.

In addition, there is a removable cook lid on top.

Specifications

Dimensions: 25¾" high x 36" deep
Door opening: 8" x 10½"
Firebox size: 15¾" high x 11¾" wide x 23½" deep
Top opening: 11¾" x 12½"
Smoke collar: 6"
Price: Approximately $199
Material: Cast iron
Weight: 130 lbs.
Guarantee: Unconditionally guaranteed for 10 years

THE ARCTIC BOX HEATER

The Arctic Box Heater is made by the Washington Stove Works from their own original 100-year-old patterns, in continuous production since the stove was first designed.

One of several box stoves made by this company, the Arctic has a large front door for front-loading, as well as a handy, swing-out top for loading whole logs when refueling. There are two removable stove-top lids for cooking, and a hearth panel that lifts up for easy ash cleanout. The Arctic will burn both wood and coal.

Specifications

Dimensions: 26½″ high x 15¼″ wide x 34½″ deep

Firebox size: 12″ high x 10″ wide x 23″ deep

Pipe collar: 6″

Price: Approximately $132

Materials: Cast iron

Weight: 110 lbs.

UNITED STATES STOVE BOXWOOD

An unpretentious box stove with clean, simple lines. The Boxwood is made of heavy-gauge steel that won't crack under extreme heat or rough handling. A two-pot cooking top lifts off for easy top loading of wood; adjustable-draft slide door provides heat control.

This is a stove meant for small heating jobs—a garage, basement, or average-sized room. It is also available in a larger model.

Specifications

Dimensions: 24½″ high x 15″ wide x 34½″ deep

Firebox size: 15″ high x 12″ wide x 26″ deep

Flue size: 6″

Price: Approximately $74.50

Materials: 8- to 10-gauge plate steel

Shipping weight: 95 lbs.

REGINALD BOX STOVE

Named after the Dane-King of Waterford, the Reginald is an airtight, cast-iron box stove made in Ireland by Waterford Ironfounders.

The 16-inch logs burn front to back "like a cigar." Side and top protection baffles circulate volatiles inside the firebox to produce greater heat and more complete combustion; draft is controlled by vent on tightly sealed door.

Top surface is suitable for cooking either in pots and pans or on a specially ground lid which can be used as a griddle —for making pancakes and similar foods directly on the cooking surface.

This is an exceptionally efficient stove, which will heat a considerable area in spite of its comparatively small size.

Specifications

Dimensions: 25″ high x 12.8″ wide x 18.3″ deep

Firebox: Takes 16″ logs

Flue outlet collar: 5″

Prices: Approximately $259.50, assembled; approximately $229.50, do-it-yourself kit

Material: Cast iron

Weight: 114 lbs.

Shipping weight: 120 lbs.

Heating capacity: 4,766 cubic feet

Thermostatically Controlled Heaters

ASHLEY IMPERIAL C-60 THERMOSTATICALLY CONTROLLED HEATER

Ashley heaters have been in continuous production for about 100 years. In the early part of the twentieth century they introduced automatic heating to American homes, and they still supply parts for models discontinued thirty years ago.

The Ashley Imperial is a deluxe heater with a handsome steel cabinet. It heats 4 to 5 average rooms with a thermostatically controlled system described as down draft. The combustion air is introduced at the front of the firebox, after being preheated, so the flow to the flue is across the fire. There is a patented secondary air intake. You dial the heat you want to maintain.

A 5.5-cubic-foot firebox holds 100 pounds of wood at one filling, so that the heater can operate up to 12 hours without refueling.

The cabinet is mahogany baked enamel on steel, with a lift-off top for emergency cooking. The front of the cabinet is metallic mesh, which is functional as well as decorative since it permits greater radiation. An accessory side door conceals the firebox door and a separate airtight ash removal door and pan.

Specifications

Dimensions: 36″ high x 35¼″ wide x 21¼″ deep

Firebox size: 5.5 cubic feet, takes logs up to 24″

Fuel door size: 13⅜″ x 9¾″

Height to bottom of collar: 24¼″

Flue collar: 6″

Color and price: Mahogany enamel cabinet with gold trim and gold-tone metallic mesh; approximately $279

Materials: Sheet steel body; cast-iron firebox liner, grate, flue collar, feed and ash doors

Shipping weight: 267 lbs.

Option: Warm-floor blower

Heating capacity: 4 to 5 average rooms

Warranty: 1 year

ATLANTA AUTOMATIC WOOD-BURNING HEATER 24 WGE

Thermostatically controlled heater with directional louvers on top to increase circulation of warm air. Handy airtight door on side opens for easy ash removal.

Since cold floors can cut down on the comfort of an otherwise well-heated room, an optional blower attachment is available that is easily installed, manually controlled, and is said to deliver 150 cfm of warm air to the floor.

Specifications

Cabinet dimensions: 35″ long x 36½″ high

Firebox size: 21″ high x 12″ wide x 24½″ long

Height to center of flue: 27″

Flue size: 6″

Fuel door: 10″ x 13½″

Colors and price: Beige-coppertone cabinet; approximately $475.95

Materials: Steel with cast-iron lining; asbestos-lined fire and ash doors

Shipping weight: 317 lbs.

UNITED STATES STOVE WONDERWOOD

A thermostatically controlled circulator with a large-capacity firebox that provides "nighttime" heating with one loading of wood. No electricity is needed to operate this unit unless the optional blower is used; otherwise a thermostat operates the draft control according to your setting. Fully welded construction and specially gasketed doors.

Specifications

Dimensions: 33″ high x 19″ wide x 32½″ deep

Firebox size: Takes wood 24″ long

Flue size: 6″

Price: Approximately $262.50

Materials: All plate steel; 12-gauge steel firebox, firebrick lined; cast-iron grates; enameled outside jacket

Shipping weight: 220 lbs.

Heating capacity: 50,000 to 60,000 Btu's

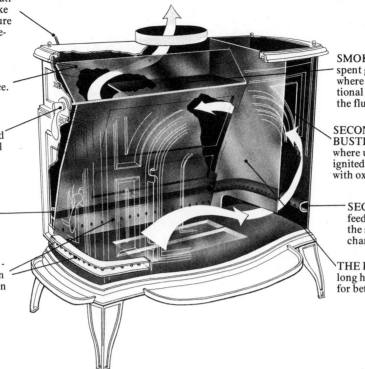

THERMOSTAT - automatically controls oxygen intake during combustion to assure even heat production at desired level.

DAMPER - lowered it permits use as a fireplace.

DAMPER CONTROL HANDLE - all handles and accent hardware are nickel plated.

SECONDARY AIR ENTRANCE PORT.

PRIMARY AIR PORTS - disperse preheated oxygen evenly into the combustion zone.

SMOKE SHELF - directs spent gases into top chamber where they give off additional heat before exiting up the flue.

SECONDARY COMBUSTION CHAMBER - where unburned volatiles are ignited when combined with oxygen.

SECONDARY AIR TUBE - feeds preheated oxygen to the secondary combustion chamber.

THE BAFFLE - creates 60" long horizontal flame path for better heat transferal.

DEFIANT PARLOR STOVE

A stove that is quite literally in a class by itself.

The Defiant is a Franklin in that it will operate in a horizontal combustion mode with a view of the open fire. With the cast-iron construction, it can also function as an airtight, Scandinavian-style box stove, operating in an updraft combustion mode. It is a thermostatically controlled stove—the only cast-iron one on the market so far as I have been able to determine.

It has the longest flame path of any stove made; it is larger and heavier than the finest imported box stoves and will accept logs up to 26" long. Because it can be both front- and side-loaded, it allows you to use large logs without splitting them—a real work saver—and a full wood load can produce heat for as long as 18 hours. Logs burn from the bottom and are gravity-fed into the flame area.

The Defiant is molded by hand in sand and finished by hand, and each stove is assembled by a single person from start to finish. Photo shows David Syme, sales manager, in the assembly room, working on a Defiant.

There is an 8- by 6-inch removable cast-iron lid, ground like a frying pan. It works very efficiently as a griddle and lifts off for cleaning. In addition, top can be used for standard cooking in pots.

Specifications

Dimensions: 32" high x 34" wide x 22" deep; depth without hearth, 18"; legs 7¼"

Firebox size: 25" high x 26" wide x 6" deep; holds approximately 60 lbs. of wood

Stovepipe size: 8"

Price: Approximately $495, including fire screen

Material: Cast iron

Weight: 320 lbs.

Heating capacity: 10,000 cubic feet; rated 55,000 Btu's

David Syme of Vermont Castings working on a Defiant.

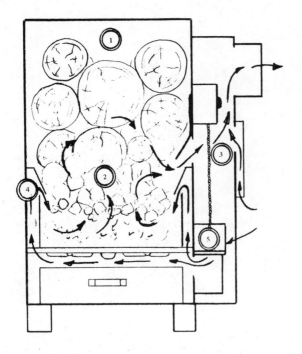

RITEWAY THERMOSTATICALLY CONTROLLED HEATER #37

First of all, do not be put off by the photograph of this fine heater. Riteway is so proud of their stoves that they show them without the modern cabinet that will enclose them in your living room; they feel that the cabinet is basically decorative, and that what you are paying for in a wood heater is the innards.

This model holds more wood than any thermostatically controlled heater on the market—the firebox is a full 7½ cubic feet. It has a very effective combustion system (see diagram), regulated by a bimetallic thermostat. It requires loading only once every 12 hours—minimum—and burns so completely that you need to empty the ash pan only two or three times a month.

Specifications

Cabinet dimensions: 42″ high x 27″ wide x 37″ long

Firebox size: 7½ cubic feet; takes 24″ long wood, up to 12″ thick

Floor to top of collar: 36″

Pipe collar: 6″

Fuel door size: 12″ x 12″

Price: Approximately $516, with cabinet; price includes magnetic damper, Riteheat regulator, poker, ash pan, and grate shaker

Materials: Heavy-gauge steel (14- and 10-gauge body); cast-iron brick retainers, flue baffle, direct draft damper, draft louvers and grates, asbestos-lined fire and ash doors

Cabinet colors: Two-tone mahogany and gold, or black and gold

Warranty: 1 year

Shipping weight: 400 lbs.

Heating capacity: 4 to 8 rooms; rated at 73,000 Btu's

SHENANDOAH THERMOSTATICALLY CONTROLLED HEATER R-75

A versatile, all-purpose heater; excellent supplementary heater in combination with your central heating system, or as the only heat source for small home or cottage.

Bimetallic thermostat is located on the door, where it is easy to adjust; 9-inch firebrick lining prolongs life of jacket, assists burning, and retains heat when fire dies down. Primary and controlled secondary air results in a very efficient burn.

Specifications

Dimensions: 35″ high, 24″ diameter
Firebox size: 23″ high, 21″ diameter
Loading door opening: 12″ x 13″
Pipe collar: 6″
Price: Approximately $205.33
Materials: 11-gauge steel top, 18-gauge steel jacket; firebrick lining; cast-iron grate
Weight: 164 lbs.
Shipping weight: 178 lbs.
Heating capacity: 2 to 5 rooms

SHENANDOAH THERMOSTATICALLY CONTROLLED HEATER R-76

High-quality, efficient cabinet heater, air-tight and thermostatically controlled. Heavy-gauge steel used throughout; 11-gauge top, 18-gauge jacket, with 9-inch firebrick liner and cast-iron grate. The bimetallic thermostat eliminates fire-tending to a large extent; heater will burn up to 12 hours on one load; easily holds fire overnight with hot bed of coals left to start fire quickly in the morning.

Most of the air is supplied to the fire as primary air through the cast-iron grate. Secondary air is supplied as needed. The air first passes through the preheating channel to the thermostatically controlled damper, then enters the firebox as primary air through the cast-iron grate. As the fire calls for secondary air, the air passes between the grate and door into the upper part of the burning chamber.

Ash pan below the grate makes it possible to collect ashes without waiting for fire to go out or die down.

Specifications

Dimensions: 36″ high x 24″ wide x 35½″ long

Firebox size: 23″ high x 15″ wide x 26″ long

Fill door size: 13″ x 12″

Side door opening: 16″ x 26″

Baffle at top of door opening: 4½″

Pipe collar: 6″

Color and price: Black porcelain enamel jacket with gold trim; approximately $310

Materials: Heavy, black iron body, firebrick liner, cast-iron grate

Shipping weight: 260 lbs.

Heating capacity: 4 to 6 rooms

WOOD KING AUTOMATIC 6600

A rugged, thermostatically controlled heater with handy top-loading feature. The top swings open for easy refueling.

Bimetal control on large front feed door lets you dial the amount of heat you want stove to maintain, holds fire up to 14 hours on one load of wood.

Specifications

Overall height: 44″
Firebox: 19″ high x 25″ long
Price: Approximately $180.95
Materials: Cast-iron top and bottom; heavy-duty steel liner
Shipping weight: 170 lbs.

Other Wood Stoves

B & M POTBELLY STOVES

These stoves are called B & M stoves because they were originally made for the Boston & Maine Railroad to use for heating their cabooses and railroad stations. They are also the type of stoves around which, in small villages, the town philosophers gathered to dispense their cracker-barrel wisdom.

The B & M stoves were manufactured at the Portland Stove Foundry in Portland, Maine—and they still are. The Portland Foundry, established in 1877, makes these stoves just as they always have; of 100 percent cast iron, hand-cast into sand molds and then hand-built.

There are three B & M stoves available; the one shown in the photograph and described in the specifications is #3, the middle-sized model, with a handy rail for drying wet socks, for instance, or for propping up one's feet. The stoves will burn wood or coal.

Specifications

Dimensions: 38″ high, 17″ diameter
Firepot: 15″
Smoke collar: 6″
Price: Approximately $499
Material: Cast iron
Weight: 234 lbs.
Guarantee: Unconditionally guaranteed for 10 years

BETTER 'N BEN'S

As the name implies, this stove is a great improvement over Ben Franklin's Pennsylvanian Fire-place. It is called a fireplace stove because a see-through screen makes it possible to view the open fire. It is designed to be placed directly in front of the fireplace opening, which is then closed with a panel and the stove vented into the existing fireplace flue. The panel fastens safely, securely, and easily within minutes, without masonry alterations.

Highly efficient in its class, Better 'N Ben will heat safely through the night—10 to 14 hours—on one load of seasoned hardwood. The University of Connecticut, in its Fall 1974 Energy Seminar, rated these stoves "sturdy, economical, safe, easy to install."

Broad top provides large, useful cooking surface.

Specifications

Dimensions: Standard back panel: 34½″ high x 42″ wide; three other sizes are available

Firebox size: 18″ high x 18″ wide x 24″ deep

Door opening: 9″ x 13″

Price: Approximately $249 to $269, depending on size of fireplace opening; price includes heat deflector

Option: See-through screen for viewing the fire

Material: 11-gauge black iron (low-carbon steel)

Weight: 143 lbs.

Shipping weight: 150 lbs.

Heating capacity: Over 10,000 cubic feet

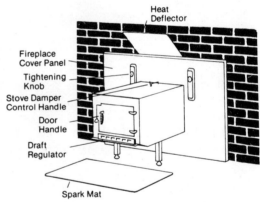

FISHER STOVE

There is nothing else like the Fisher Stove —it is a truly unique design. The Fisher Stove Works in Oregon describes it as a heater, a cookstove, and a trash burner, but it functions in each of these areas in its own special way.

The uniqueness of the Fisher is due to the fact that the top has two levels. Inside, within the firebox, the two levels create air turbulence because the lower front level has a cooler temperature than the higher back level. Further, the exhaust is 2″ lower than the top, which helps retain more heat in the stove; and the venting pipe actually extends 3″ into the stove, which allows greater combustion and lower ash residue. In addition, the baffle design prevents heat loss up the chimney. In tests in Pennsylvania, the Fisher was rated 76 percent efficient.

Because of the difference in inside temperatures, the cooking surface temperatures are also different and provide great flexibility in use.

The Fisher has easy draft controls, and the door has a fitted U channel and a wedge-lock feature that creates a tight seal. The Fisher will hold a fire up to 24 hours.

Specifications

Dimensions: 28″ high x 18″ wide x 32″ deep
Firebox size: Takes wood up to 30″
Price: Approximately $350
Materials: ¼″ and ⁵⁄₁₆″ MSPL steel, all-welded construction; firebrick lined
Weight: Approximately 410 lbs.
Heating capacity: 2,000 square feet

HOME ATLANTIC
PARLOR STOVE

The Home Atlantic Parlor Stove is a handsome cast-iron stove that has been used to heat parlors since 1910, when it was first cast by the Portland Stove Foundry. It is available with a return flue that recirculates the volatiles that are normally lost up the chimney, thus increasing heat output and slowing down the fire. When a direct draft is wanted—as when starting a fire, for instance—the return flue can be opened.

The decorative urn on top is not functional.

Specifications

Dimensions: Height to top of
   ornament: 37″; at base, approximately:
   22½″ long, 19″ deep
Firebox size: 12½″ x 18″; takes 18″ logs
Smoke pipe size: 6″
Price: Approximately $399
Material: Cast iron
Weight: 174 lbs.
Guarantee: Unconditionally guaranteed
   for 10 years

TEMPWOOD

Tempwood is a stove that works on the downdraft principle. Air enters the firebox through two drafts positioned on the stove top, and the wood is top-loaded. The fire is built backward—the chunk wood or logs go in first, then kindling, and finally, on top just under the draft openings, wadded newspaper. Since the fire burns from the top down, no grate is needed, and the top drafts produce a "blow-torch" effect in the firebox, which results in nearly total combustion of the fuel, with minimal accumulation of ashes. Fire lasts 12 to 14 hours on a burn, without refueling.

It is a safe stove because there are no side or front openings from which a spark can escape. The stove is fully welded and airtight. A large removable stove lid on top is handy for cooking.

Installed in front of, and vented into an existing fireplace, the flue pipe doesn't show.

As to heating efficiency, John Notsley of Tempwood writes: "I personally heat my six-room ranch home with one Tempwood, and last year burned 5½ cords of wood. I normally use 1,100 gallons of fuel oil, so the savings to me was great."

Specifications

Dimensions: 28″ high x 28″ wide x 18″ deep

Firebox size: 25″ x 14″

Lid opening size: 11″

Flue size: 6″

Price: Approximately $249

Materials: All steel (except for stove lid): 11-gauge top, 13-gauge body, steel liner; 11″ cast-iron lid

Weight: 132 lbs.

Heating capacity: Rated 60,000 Btu's

WASHINGTON PARLOR STOVE

The design of the Washington Parlor Stove is truly antique—in fact, it is still made from the original hand-carved patterns that the Washington Stove Works first used in the last century.

It burns both wood and charcoal and has side- and front-loading doors, as well as a removable top. In addition, the top has two removable stove lids for cooking.

If preferred, this stove can be installed directly on the hearth, within the fireplace, by ordering it specifically without base or legs.

It comes in five models but they are all the same size and shape; the difference lies in the trim packs available. The trim packs become progressively elaborate; Model V, for instance, includes a nickel-plated swing top, foot rail, top rail, and door frame. Model IV, illustrated in the photograph, has a nickel-plated foot rail, top rail, and door frame.

Specifications

Dimensions: 31¼″ high x 25½″ wide x 22½″ deep; height does not include base frame or legs
Front opening: 12″ x 6½″
Top opening: 18½″ x 10½″
Side opening: 14″ x 8″
Pipe collar: 6″
Price: Approximately $335, without trim
Spark guard: 13¼″ wide x 10½″ high
Material: Cast iron
Weight: 180 lbs.
Options: 4 trim packs

Fireplaces

AEROHEATER

Invented by Alex Moncrieff-Yeates, the Aeroheater is a custom-fitted fireplace that slides into an existing fireplace and can even be easily removed, if desired.

It has a triple-steel-wall construction with a vortex heat exchanger, so that room air is heated by passing over metal surfaces heated by the fireplace fire. Because of its design, heated air flows into the room from upper ducts while smoke goes up the flue; the room air and fire air are kept separate by steel walls at all times.

Susan Yeats writes of her own experience with the Aeroheater: "The house . . . was brick, not terribly well insulated, but with storm windows, and used typically 1,200 to 1,500 gallons of oil a winter. . . . From mid-winter 1975 (January) to June 1976, we used about 175 gallons and the bill was less than $75. Our wood bill was also less than when we burned just the fireplace and oil burner. We burned about 2 cords a winter, including demonstrating the unit in the summer.

"Plus the fact, that I was *warm* and so were the cats!"

The Aeroheater is also available as a free-standing fireplace.

Specifications

Dimensions: Depending on the size of your fireplace

Firebox size: Holds from 16 to 24 lbs. of wood (depending on size of unit)

Colors and price: Black, red, and yellow; approximately $400

Materials: Welded and riveted steel plates

Weight: Approximately 100 lbs.

Heating capacity: 28,000 to 40,000 Btu's; will heat an entire single-level home

THE FREE HEAT MACHINE CIRCULATING FIREPLACE

How it works

This unique heat exchanger takes in cool room air via quiet dual fans. The cold room air is forced through a series of C-shaped, hollow, low-carbon, cold-rolled steel tubes, $1\frac{1}{2}$ inches in diameter (which also serve as a grate to hold the wood), so that air passes under, behind, and then up over the fire toward the room. The heat from the fire warms the cold air brought into the tubes, and the two fans then gently blow it back into the room at the rate of 160 cubic feet per minute. The smoke and gases from the fire in the fireplace are vented up the chimney, as usual, but clean, heated air comes into the room over the top of the fire.

Because the tubes deliver such a high volume of air, they are kept much cooler than those in units with smaller blowers, or no blowers at all. Their life—7 to 10 years—is consequently longer.

To select the correct model to fit your fireplace, measure the height, depth, and rear width of the firebox (the inside dimensions) of your fireplace.

Specifications

What it includes: Complete unit (as shown in photograph) with tubes and two blowers, ash pan (just slide it into existing fireplace and plug in), wire-mesh spark screen

Sizes: 4 sizes available

Material: Low-carbon, cold-rolled steel

Overall width at front: $46\frac{5}{8}''$

Options: Glass doors, manual heat control, top panel extension (if needed)

Prices: From approximately $279, depending on size

HEATFORM CIRCULATING FIREPLACE

How it works

The Heatform is a double-walled, warm air-circulating fireplace unit. Air chambers surrounding the firebox and upper-throat capture and circulate through the home a large percentage of heat lost to the chimney by the ordinary fireplace.

Cool room air is drawn into large air-chamber inlets on each side of unit. Air moves back to the main heating chamber, directed by two special air baffles. The cool air becomes increasingly heated as it contacts and rises up the hot firebox wall; a mass of warm air flows through the "super heat tubes" and around each side of the throat's enclosed upper heating chamber.

Heated air then flows through 4-inch-diameter heat-flue tubes and out the main hot-air grill above the fireplace. It can also be ducted right and left from alternate outlets in the upper firebox.

As a result, the Heatform heats both through radiation—from the open fire—and through convection—through warm air-circulation outlets.

Specifications

What it includes: Heavy steel firebox plus a hinged friction damper to control heat, smoke dome, and preformed throat chamber (see diagram)

Sizes: 13 sizes in 3 different styles available

Fuel: Any fireplace fuel may be used

Materials: Heavy-gauge steel

Warranty: 20-year limited warranty; the most comprehensive in the market for this class of fireplace; parts are covered for 20 years, labor for 10 years

Prices: Approximately $199 to $534

Weight: From 159 to 360 lbs.

Heating capacity: 4,300 to 9,500 Btu's, depending on style and size; ratings based on 20 degrees above zero

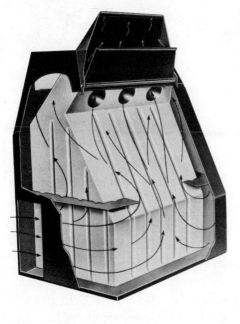

JØTUL PREFABRICATED FIREBOX: SYSTEM 15

A work of art that can be a traditional fireplace, a free-standing fireplace on legs, or even a box stove. The heart of the system is Norwegian sculpture, by a well-known Norwegian artist, which is in the form of a cast-iron firebox or fireplace lining.

The versatility of System 15 lies in its components—there are thirteen of them —allowing innumerable variations of design and layout. Even more components are available on special order.

Installed as a fireplace lining in a custom-built traditional fireplace, for instance, System 15 provides a heating chamber behind the cast-iron firebox. Cold air enters beneath the fire, is led up behind the firebox, then delivered as heated air back into the room through vents above the fireplace; this doubles the heating efficiency of the traditional fireplace.

MALM IMPERIAL CAROUSEL

A free-standing fireplace with a firebox enclosed in tempered glass, which gives a clear view of the fire from any angle. Combustion-created heat currents twist upward inside a wall of incoming air and create beautiful "spinning" flames. Comes in black and a number of brilliant porcelain colors.

Specifications

Dimensions: 98″ overall height x 40″ wide x 40″ deep; height of unit: 54″

Flue size: 8″

Colors: Matte black

Standard: burnt orange, burnt red, burnt gold, white, harvest gold porcelain

Optional: burnt green, zinnia, coppertone, turquoise, blue porcelain

Prices: Approximately $579.50 for black; more for porcelain colors

Shipping weight: 250 lbs.

THERMOGRATE

Thermograte is a **C**-shaped, tubular-steel fireplace grate that provides heat from convection as well as the normal fireplace heat from radiation. Cold air is brought in under the burning wood, up the back of the fireplace, and over the top of the flaming logs to return warm air into the room.

According to Thermograte, tests show that a Thermograte unit, replacing an ordinary cast-iron grate, will produce as many as 25,000 Btu's per hour. Adding an optional, auxiliary blower to this unit will increase the heat output to approximately 40,000 Btu's per hour. An ordinary fireplace fire is said to produce about 6,000 to 8,000 Btu's per hour.

The Thermograte line includes 28 models in a full range of sizes to assure accurate fit for nearly all fireplaces. Accuracy of fit is necessary for maximum effectiveness of this system, which utilizes the principles of natural convection to produce hot-air circulation even without supplementary blowers—in other words, if your electric power should fail, you would still get a great deal of benefit from this heating system.

Thermograte fireplaces will not only burn logs, branches, and lumber scraps, but also newspapers and other burnable trash.

Specifications

Dimensions: 28 models, full range of sizes

Material: 14-gauge steel tubes, .083" thick, all-welded construction

Price: Depending on size, from approximately $59.95 to $194.95

Shipping weight: Depending on size, 31 to 119 lbs.

Optional: Blower

Warranty: 2-year, limited-performance warranty

Furnaces

BELLWAY HI-TEMP HEATERS, FURNACES, BOILERS

Putting in a wood-burning furnace doesn't necessarily mean ripping out your present heating system. The Bellway comes complete with controls and casings—ready to connect to your chimney and heating system. It will heat alone or will combine with your present oil, coal, or electric unit, if desired. If used in combination, your present system—an oil burner, for example—is on standby and will kick in only if the wood supply runs out.

Bellways are thermostatically controlled and will maintain even heat in your home—up to 10 rooms—for 10 hours in 0-degree weather without any further attention on your part after loading. They will burn green or dry wood, garbage, old paper, and similar fuel. Because of their design, wood is placed in the top section where it dries out, feeding down by gravity, as needed, to the high-temperature burner in the lower section, thus minimizing problems associated with burning green wood.

Heavy-duty heaters with automatic controls are made in three models that take 24-inch logs; furnaces and boilers come in four models that take 24-, 36-, or 48-inch logs.

They will heat houses of 3 to 10 rooms —customers report using the system to heat swimming pools along with their homes—in complete comfort.

Bellways have heavy-steel construction, are Mig-welded and smoke tight, and are rated like oil burners so far as Btu's are concerned. All are sold direct and manufactured to order.

NEWMAC COMBINATION FURNACE

The Newmac Combination Furnace, imported from Canada, burns both wood and oil. However, unlike other combination furnaces, it is specifically designed to burn the wood in an airtight chamber separated from the chamber in which the oil is burned. Because of this special design feature, it approaches 60 percent efficiency when burning wood. Combustion is so complete that users report having to remove ashes (through the feed door) only once or twice during the entire heating season—negating the need for, and eliminating the problems caused by, an ash pit door in an airtight furnace.

The Newmac switches from wood to oil automatically, as supply of fuel and temperature setting indicates. It has twin 10-inch blowers for quiet, efficient operation and can be used with your existing hot-air system; or with the aid of simple duct work, it can be installed to provide hot-air distribution throughout the house —for instance, in homes which may now be heated electrically or by hot water.

The Newmac firebox has a heavy stainless steel liner and will take up to 24-inch logs through a 17½-square-inch door.

It is manufactured in four sizes with a Btu output ranging from 113,000 to 168,000. Prices start at approximately $1,500.

Warranties include 1 year on the controls; 2 years on the Carlin burner; 5 years on the replacement steel liner; and a 10-year full warranty on the heat exchanger. A stainless steel tank for domestic hot water is optional.

RITEWAY FURNACES

Riteway furnaces are like all furnaces meant for central heating. They are multifuel, which means they can efficiently burn wood or coal as well as oil or gas—even bottled gas, if that is what is most easily available in your area—in the same combustion chamber.

If wood or coal is used as the primary fuel, you simply set the oil or gas burner thermostat 2 to 3 degrees lower than the wood/coal thermostat. If the wood/coal supply in the combustion chamber fails to maintain the temperature desired, the oil/gas burner automatically kicks in and maintains the thermostat setting—no one has to be there to make the switch from one fuel to the other. (This same system works equally well if oil/gas is the primary fuel.)

Riteway has several models of furnaces, from approximately $1,950. The more expensive the furnace, the larger it is and the greater its fuel and heating capacity. Domestic hot-water heaters are optional with all models.

If you aren't sure what size you need for your home, Riteway's engineering department will help you figure it out. However, most purchasers of wood-burning furnaces will work through a local contractor. If you write directly to the company, you will be better informed when you talk to your contractor.

Riteway warranties are as follows: 1 year for firebrick and cast-iron combustion flue; 5 years for furnaces and boilers. Electrical components are limited to the warranty offered by the respective manufacturers.

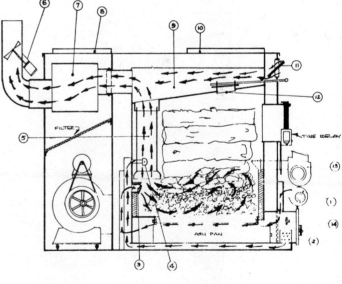

THE THERMO-CONTROL
FURNACE #500

This thermostatically controlled furnace can be installed to operate as a stove, or to fit into your present heating system. For a hot-water system, specify Thermo-Control #500W; it comes equipped with factory-installed water pipes and furnishes domestic hot water as well as hot-water heating. For hot-air heating, specify Thermo-Control #500A (see photograph).

According to the manufacturer, customers report that they receive 24 hours of comfortable household heat from a single load of fuel. If used with your existing furnace, the thermostat will kick it on if the wood level allows the temperature to drop below your setting.

Specifications

Dimensions: 32″ high x 24″ wide x 36″ deep
Door size: 18″ x 21″
Price: Model 500, approximately $329.95
Materials: Heavy gauge ¼″ and ³⁄₁₆″ hot-rolled black steel; firebrick lined
Shipping weight: Approximately 360 lbs.

Appendix

WHERE TO BUY
WOOD-BURNING STOVES

Here is a partial list of manufacturers, representatives, and importers of wood-burning stoves. An asterisk (*) indicates stoves not described in the catalog. These companies will be glad to furnish you with the name of a distributor in your area.

Aeroheator Co.
P.O. Box 1461
Springfield, Virginia 22151

Arctic Box Heater
(see Washington Stove Works)

Ashley Imperial Automatic Heater Co.
1604 17th Avenue, S.W.
P.O. Box 730
Sheffield, Alabama 35660

*Athens Stove Works
P.O. Box 10
Athens, Tennessee 37303

Atlanta Stove Works
Krog Street, P.O. Box 5254
Atlanta, Georgia 30307

*Atlantic Stove Works
(see Washington Stove Works)

*Autocart Corp.
New Athens, Illinois 62264

*Automatic Draft & Stove Co.
Lynchburg, Virginia 24505

Bellway Hi-Temp
Bellway Manufacturing
Perley C. Bell
Grafton, Vermont 05146

Ben Franklin
(see King Products Division)

B & M Potbelly Stoves
(see Portland Stove Foundry)

Better 'N Ben's
C & D Distributors, Inc.
P.O. Box 766
Old Saybrook, Connecticut 06475

*Birmingham Stove & Range Co.
Box 2593
Birmingham, Alabama 35202

*Bow & Arrow Stove Co.
14 Arrow Street
Cambridge, Massachusetts 02138

*Brown Stove Works, Inc.
Cleveland, Tennessee 37311

*Chappee French Wood-Burning Stoves
Preston Distributing Co.
Whidden Street
Lowell, Massachusetts 01852

*Dawson Manufacturing Co.
Shaker Road
Enfield, Connecticut 06082

Defiant Parlor Stove
Vermont Casting, Inc.
Box 126
Prince Street
Randolph, Vermont 05060

Eagle Franklin Stove
(see Portland Stove Works)

*Edison Potbelly Stoves
Edison Stove Works
469 Raritan Center
Edison, New Jersey 08817

*Edwards Manufacturing Co.
529-49 Eggleston Avenue
Cincinnati, Ohio 45202

*Fire-A-Lator
(see Superior Fireplace Co.)

Fisher Stove Works
135 Commercial
Springfield, Oregon 97447

The Free Heat Machine
Aquappliances, Inc.
135 Sunshine Lane
San Marcos, California 92069

Heatform Circulating Fireplace
(see Superior Fireplace Co.)

*Heatilator
Vega Industries
P.O. Box 409
Mt. Pleasant, Iowa 52641

*The Heidelberger (Germany)
Hoskin Diversified Industries (HDI)
Schoolhouse Farm
Etna, New Hampshire 03750

Home Atlantic Parlor Stove
(see Portland Stove Foundry)

*Hoval Combination Hot Water Boiler
(see S/A Distributors)

Jøtul Stoves
Kristia Associates
343 Forest Avenue
P.O. Box 1118
Portland, Maine 04104

King Products Division
Martin Industries
P.O. Box 730
Sheffield, Alabama 35660

Lange Stoves
(see Scandinavian Stoves, Inc.)

*Locke Stove Co.
114 West 11th Street
Kansas City, Missouri 64105

*Majestic Free-Standing Fireplaces &
Majestitherm Fireplace System
The Majestic Co.
Huntington, Indiana 46750

Malm Fireplaces, Inc.
368 Yolanda Avenue
Santa Rosa, California 95404

*Monarch Kitchen Appliances Division
Malleable Iron Range Co.
Beaver Dam, Wisconsin 53916

Morsø Stoves
Southport Stoves
248 Tolland Street
East Hartford, Connecticut 06108

Newmac Combination Furnace
(see S/A Distributors)

Olympic Franklin
(see Washington Stove Works)

Portland Stove Foundry, Inc.
57 Kennebec Street
Portland, Maine 04104

*Preway Prefab Fireplaces
Wisconsin Rapids, Wisconsin 54494

Queen Atlantic
(see Portland Stove Foundry)

*Reeves-Bowman Division
Cyclops Corp.
Dover, Ohio 44622

Reginald Box Stove
(see S/A Distributors)

Riteway Manufacturing Co.
P.O. Box 6
Harrisonburg, Virginia 22801

S/A Distributors
    700 East Water Street
    Suite 730 Midtown Plaza
    Syracuse, New York 13210

*Sam Daniels Furnace
    Sam Daniels Co.
    U.S. Route 2
    Box 868
    Montpelier, Vermont 05602

Scandinavian Stoves, Inc.
    Box 72
    Alstead, New Hampshire 03602

Shenandoah Heaters
    Shenandoah Manufacturing Co., Inc.
    P.O. Box 839
    Harrisonburg, Virginia 22801

*Southern Co-Operative Foundry Co.
    P.O. Box 69
    Rome, Georgia 30161

Stanley Kitchen Range
    (see S/A Distributors)

Superior Fireplace Co.
    4325 Artesia Avenue
    Fullerton, California 92633

Tempwood
    Mohawk Industries, Inc.
    173 Howland Avenue
    Adams, Massachusetts 01220

Thermo-Control Wood Stoves
    General Engineering Building
    Central Bridge, New York 12035

Thermograte Enterprises, Inc.
    51 Iona Lane
    St. Paul, Minnesota 55117

Tiba Cooking Range
    (see Scandinavian Stoves, Inc.)

*Trolla Stoves
    (see Portland Stove Foundry)

United States Stove Co.
    South Pittsburg, Tennessee 37380

Washington Stove Works
    P.O. Box 687
    Everett, Washington 98201

Wood King
    (see King Products Division)

Characteristics of Woods for Fireplace Use*

Species	Ease of Starting	Coaling Qualities	Sparks	Fragrance
Apple	Poor	Excellent	Few	Excellent
Ash	Fair	Good	Few	Slight
Beech	Poor	Good	Few	Slight
Birch, white	Good	Good	Moderate	Slight
Cherry	Poor	Excellent	Few	Excellent
Cedar	Excellent	Poor	Many	Good
Douglas Fir	Good	Low	Many	Good
Elm	Fair	Good	Very Few	Fair
Hemlock	Good	Low	Many	Good
Hickory	Fair	Excellent	Moderate	Slight
Locust, black	Poor	Excellent	Very Few	Slight
Maple, sugar	Poor	Excellent	Few	Good
Oak, red	Poor	Excellent	Few	Fair
Pine, white or yellow	Excellent	Poor	Moderate	Good

One interesting point is that green white ash burns fairly well, as the moisture content is lower than other species.

*Courtesy of Maine Bureau of Forestry and School of Forestry, Oregon State University

Effects of Seasoning of Hardwoods on Moisture Content and Heat Value*

Condition of Wood	Moisture Content (% of oven-dried weight)	Relative Heat Value (% of value for air-dry)
Green in fall, winter, or spring	78	65
Green in summer	64	—
Trees leaf-felled in summer after 2 weeks	45	—
Spring wood seasoned 3 months	35	85
Spring wood seasoned 6 months	30	93
Dry wood seasoned 12 months	25	100

* Courtesy of the Society for the Protection of New Hampshire Forests

Importance of Air-Dry Wood
Approximate Fuel Values*

Species	Available Heat Units (Million Btu's/90 cu. ft. wood)		Weight (lbs./cu. ft.)	
	Air-Dry	Green	Air-Dry	Green
BEST				
Ash, white	20.0	18.0	41	48
Beech	21.8	19.7	45	54
Birch, yellow	21.3	19.4	44	57
Hickory, shagbark	25.4	23.8	51	63
Hophornbeam	24.7	23.5	—	—
Locust, black	26.5	24.4	48	58
Maple, sugar	21.8	19.6	44	56
Oak, red	21.7	19.6	44	64
white	23.9	20.4	47	63
MODERATELY GOOD				
Birch, gray	17.5	16.1	—	—
white or paper	18.2	16.7	38	50
Cherry, black	18.5	17.3	35	45
Elm, white	17.7	15.8	35	54
Maple, red	19.1	17.6	38	50
silver	17.9	16.4	33	45
Oak, Oregon white	19.1	18.1	37	47
Pine, Norway	17.8	16.8	34	42
pitch	18.5	16.4	—	—
Tamarack	19.1	18.1	37	47
POOR				
Aspen, trembling	14.1	12.1	26	43
Basswood	12.6	11.0	26	42
Butternut	14.3	12.2	27	46
Cherry, pin	14.2	13.5	—	—
Fir, balsam	13.5	11.5	25	45
Fir, Douglas	15.0	12.8	28	50
Hemlock	15.0	12.8	28	50
Maple, big leaf	14.3	12.2	27	46
Pine, white	13.3	12.1	25	36
Spruce, red	15.0	14.2	28	34
Willow, black	13.5	10.9	—	—

* Courtesy of the Society for the Protection of New Hampshire Forests and the Forest Research Laboratory School of Forestry, Oregon State University

Ratings for Firewood*

Type of Tree	Relative amount of heat	Easy to burn?	Easy to split?	Does it have heavy smoke?
HARDWOOD TREES				
Ash, red oak, white oak, beech, birch, hickory, hard maple, pecan, dogwood	High	Yes	Yes	No
Soft maple, cherry, walnut	Medium	Yes	Yes	No
Elm, sycamore, gum	Medium	Medium	No	Medium
Aspen, basswood, cottonwood, yellow-poplar	Low	Yes	Yes	Medium
SOFTWOOD TREES				
Southern yellow pine, Douglas fir	High	Yes	Yes	Yes
Cypress, redwood	Medium	Medium	Yes	Medium
White cedar, western red cedar, eastern red cedar	Medium	Yes	Yes	Medium
Eastern white pine, western white pine, sugar pine, ponderosa pine, true firs	Low	Medium	Yes	Medium
Tamarack, larch	Medium	Yes	Yes	Medium
Spruce	Low	Yes	Yes	Medium

* Courtesy of USDA Forest Service

Recommended Dimensions for Fireplaces and Size of Flue Lining Required*

Size of fireplace opening			Minimum width of back wall	Height of vertical back wall	Height of inclined back wall	Size of flue lining required	
Width	Height	Depth				Standard rectangular (outside dimensions)	Standard round (inside diameter)
w	h	d	c	a	b		
Inches	Inches	Inches	Inches	Inches	Inches	Inches	Inches
24	24	16–18	14	14	16	8½ x 8½	10
28	24	16–18	14	14	16	8½ x 8½	10
30	28–30	16–18	16	14	18	8½ x 13	10
36	28–30	16–18	22	14	18	8½ x 13	12
42	28–32	16–18	28	14	18	13 x 13	12
48	32	18–20	32	14	24	13 x 13	15
54	36	18–20	36	14	28	13 x 18	15
60	36	18–20	44	14	28	13 x 18	15
54	40	20–22	36	17	29	13 x 18	15
60	40	20–22	42	17	30	18 x 18	18
66	40	20–22	44	17	30	18 x 18	18
72	40	22–28	51	17	30	18 x 18	18

* Courtesy of USDA, Farmers' Bulletin No. 1889

Heat Equivalents of Wood, by Species*

Wood (1 standard cord)[a]	Available heat of 1 cd. wood (Btu's)[b]	Anthracite coal (tons)[c]	No. 2 fuel oil (gallons)[d]	Natural gas (100 cu. ft.)[e]
Greatest Heat Equivalents—1 Cord = 1 Ton of Anthracite Coal (Approx.)				
Apple	23,877,000	1.09	244	298
Beech, American	21,800,000	.99	222	273
Elm, rock	23,488,000	1.07	240	294
Hickory, bitternut	23,477,000	1.07	240	293
Hickory, shagbark	24,600,000	1.12	251	308
Ironwood (hardhack)[f]	24,100,000	1.09	246	301
Locust, black	24,600,000	1.12	251	307
Oak, white	22,700,000	1.04	232	284
High Heat Equivalents—1 Cord = 9/10 Ton of Anthracite Coal (Approx.)				
Ash, white	20,000,000	.91	204	250
Birch, white	18,900,000	.86	193	236
Birch, yellow	21,300,000	.97	217	286
Cherry, black	18,770,000	.85	191	235
Maple, sugar	21,300,000	.97	217	286
Oak, red	21,300,000	.97	217	286
Walnut, black	19,500,000	.89	198	244
Moderate Heat Equivalents—1 Cord = 8/10 Ton of Anthracite Coal (Approx.)				
Ash, black	17,300,000	.79	177	216
Ash, green	18,360,000	.83	187	229
Elm, American	17,200,000	.78	176	215
Maple, red	18,600,000	.84	190	232
Maple, silver	17,000,000	.77	173	213
Pine, pitch	17,970,000	.82	183	225
Sycamore, American	17,950,000	.82	183	224
Tamarack (Eastern larch)	18,650,000	.85	190	233
Low Heat Equivalents—1 Cord = 6/10 Ton of Anthracite Coal (Approx.)				
Aspen (poplar)	12,500,000	.57	128	156
Basswood	11,700,000	.53	119	146
Butternut	12,800,000	.58	131	160
Fir, balsam	11,282,000	.51	115	141
Hemlock	13,500,000	.61	138	169
Pine, red	12,765,000	.58	130	160
Pine, white	12,022,000	.55	123	150
Spruce, red	13,632,000	.62	139	170
Willow, black	13,206,000	.60	135	165

ᵃ1 standard cord = 128 cubic feet wood and air; 80 cubic feet solid wood; 20% moisture content. 1 lb. of this wood contains 5,780 Btu (British thermal unit). (One Btu = amount of heat required to raise temperature of a pound of water through 1 degree Fahrenheit.)

ᵇIt is assumed that available heat of wood is oven-dry, or calorific value, minus loss due to moisture, minus loss due to water vapor formed, minus loss due to heat carried away in dry chimney gas. Stack temperature 450° Fahrenheit. No excess air. Efficiency of burning unit = 50 to 60%.

ᶜContains 28,000,000 Btu per ton, but available heat is only 22,000,000 Btu per ton. 1 lb. of coal contains 11,000 available Btu. Coal burned under similar conditions to wood.

ᵈ1 gallon contains 140,000 Btu, but is burned at 70% efficiency, providing 98,000 available Btu.

ᵉ100 cu. ft. = 1 therm = 100,000 Btu, but is burned at 80% efficiency, providing 80,000 available Btu.

ᶠHophornbeam, Eastern.

*Courtesy of the Cooperative Extension Services of the Northeast States